CYBERTRICKS

In a far flung future Pya, Zumi, Jafet and Trist, live in tiny Cells cared for by tutor-holos, and only communicate through their avatars. Pya narrates how the giant computer *ComCen* sends them back to 2043 A.D where they meet Rio and Charlie. But to survive in an increasingly dangerous world, six quarrelsome youngsters must come together as a team.

CYBERTRICKS

Goldie Alexander

A
FIVE SENSES
PUBLICATION

First published by
Five Senses Education Pty Ltd, 2016.
ABN 16 001 414 437
2/195 Prospect Highway,
Seven Hills NSW 2147

Printed by Five Senses Education Pty Ltd.

Cover Design by Aaron Pocock

Alexander, Goldie.
Cybertricks
ISBN 978-1-74130-888-4

Cybertricks

Part 1. ComCen

Part 2. Actuality

Part 3. Bushwise

Part 4. Gladiators

Part 5. Cybertricks

PART 1

ComCen

1

A New Assignment

As Weirwolf pads away, his wicked jaws still dripping saliva, the final score flashes on.

It states that me, Pya, won this endgame.

So I'm really cross when Zumi flings down her weapon and whines, 'That's so unfair! Why did Pya get higher grades than me?'

'It's the number of strikes that count,' I remind her. 'I managed to get in more strikes.'

I know she's about to argue...

...when suddenly Weirwolf's icy planet disappears and I'm back in Cell Q3 with Tutor-Henny hovering over me, saying, 'Pya, this exercise is now over.'

She hands me a food-tube. 'Your next assignment,' she says as I suck and swallow, 'will be to combine Archaeology with a lesson in Independence and Cooperation.'

I lean back in my chair and groan loudly.

'Time wasted, time lost,' Tutor-Henny carols. She shrinks to quarter size and squats ten centimetres above the floor. Around us, only faint lines show where my sleep-pod, food-drink tubes and wash-waste pod slide in and out of the walls. She says, 'In this new assignment all four Hatchlings will work together.'

This makes me sit up. Before I can get her to explain, she adds as if this is no big deal, '...and you'll be on your own. No Tutor-Holos will guide you.'

My chin drops. 'But...but we're never ever together. And you're always with me, even when I'm asleep...'

Brown eyes turn frosty blue. '*ComCen*'s decision is final!'

She vanishes, leaving me totally dumb-struck

'Pya, what's this all about?'

'Don't know.' I decide to ignore Zumi's last gripe. 'Tutor-Hecate still with you?'

She shakes her head.

All four Hatchlings working together!

No tutor-holos!

Nothing like this has ever happened before.

Before I can think this through, Zumi cries, 'Pya, send me your avatar.' Of course she just has to add, 'I think yours is starting to look better.'

As this is Zumi's way of saying hers is prettier than mine, I start to say something equally nasty, only *ComCen* mind-says, 'Jafet and Trist will reach you shortly. Pya and Zumi, please revise your last assignment.'

Next, our avatars are standing on a ridge above a green valley. The scent of freshly mown grass replaces my Cell's metallic odour. Wispy clouds dot blue skies. Trees, bushes and wild flowers surround us. I half close my eyes and bask in the sun's warmth. A light breeze rustles my hair. Birds sing. Bees hum. Cicadas trill.

'Wonder where this valley was?' I muse aloud.

Zumi doesn't answer. But I know she's thinking: If only we could live in a place like this.

Our avatars stroll along a riverbank bordered with weeping willows until we come to a village. We head into a park lined by shady maple trees. This leads us to a pool where huge goldfish swim from side to side, their plump bodies courting the afternoon sun. The scent of jonquils, narcissi and jasmine mingle. Bee-buzz fills the air. Birds and butterflies colour it. From here we look down on a main street straddled by a mossy stone bridge and see thatched roofs just beyond.

But soon the village starts to grow. Time speeds up. The goldfish and pool vanish. The park gradually shrinks. Tall buildings rise. Chimneys belch out fossil fuels. Trains reduce the countryside to shreds. Cars, planes and copters foul the skies. Cranes and skyscrapers block out the sun. Throngs fill the streets. Some wave banners. Soon we hear machine guns rattle. Bombs explode. Lethal chemicals fill the air. Though this can't hurt our real bodies, our avatars are moved inland to where smoke from burning forests pollutes the atmosphere. Landslides engulf whole towns. Surf pounds the coasts. Whole islands disappear. Most fauna and flora vanish. The ground lies parched and eroded. The few survivors are hungry and sick. These die in droves. Mushroom clouds fill the skies. Cities glow in a nuclear nightmare.

We know this as the coming of *The Great Disaster*.

2

The Great Disaster

'Not again,' Zumi's avatar groans. 'Why do we have to go over it again?'

Her avatar bounces around my Cell. I watch her through half closed eyes. I'm not fooled. Not for a second. I know her real body, just like mine, is sitting in a chair inside her tiny Cell. I know how much she'd really like to run and jump.

Not that we can.

You see, after *The Great Disaster*, those few survivors were moved into underground cities. Two millennia later, their descendants came down with the Great Plague. By then our ancestors had built *ComCen*, a super computer where all knowledge was stored. Those few humans that were still alive were moved into separate Cells so they couldn't infect each other. When they died, *ComCen* kept replacing them. Of these, as far as I know, only Zumi, Trist, and Jafet, only us four Hatchlings are left.

Tutor-Henny says we have been dipped in a vaccine vat to protect us from any mutating virus. 'Except for The Great Plague,' she always adds. '*ComCen* never found an antidote for The Great Plague. That's why you can meet only via your avatars.'

Cell Q3, my cell, is on Level 8, Circle 3, Great Southern Continent, Terra. Not that I have ever seen my reflection except in this Cell's metal walls. What I do know is that I have wispy white hair and the skin on my arms, legs and body is almost translucent. Those Hatchlings who live in 20,043 AD are almost too weak to do much except walk between a chair and a sleep-pod. Nor do I know what the others look like, though Tutor-Henny insists that we're almost identical.

We four who live in the same Circle, spend every waking hour working. We store facts in 'knowledge' buttons set into our skulls. Other lessons involve endgames where our avatars must fight opponents like Weirwolf and the giant Arachnida. Whenever I complain about yet another endgame, Henny says, 'They teach you to think quickly and rationally.' Her plump pretty face turns pensive. 'One day they will be useful. They may even save your life. And aren't they fun?'

I try not to groan too loudly.

'Hasn't your avatar learnt to punch, kick, throw, and hold an opponent in submission?'

I have to agree. Though my real body is small and weak, my avatar's ability to create T-Rex, an enormous lion, a ferocious wolf, a bear with metal teeth, and grossest of all, Gigantica Humanoidus, keeps improving. If we Hatchlings usually manage to beat most opponents, there's one that's just too hard. Whenever I mention the Betelgeux Shape-

Shifter to Jafet, his avatar face crumples. 'I agree.' His voice turns gloomy. 'That creature is seriously scary.'

'Have you ever defeated one?'

'No. As far as I can tell, no one has ever conquered a Shape-Shifter. Certainly Trist and Zumi have never managed, however...' he goes on in his usual way giving me one theory after another, until I say, 'What would you do if you really met one?'

He shudders, and for once is totally speechless.

***

Brooding, wishing for something different though I don't know what, I suddenly realise ComCen is mind-talking. 'Prepare to meet the rest of the team.'

I've worked with each masc before, but never with both together. Recently, I shared an assignment with Jafet on a mutant nano-virus. Partnering him is mostly okay, though when he keeps on and on and won't shut up, I stop listening.

Trist and I plotted a geological survey of the area surrounding our Circle plus a three dimensional map of the Milky Way. But it's never easy with Trist, possibly because he's never at ease with us fems. Once, we were working on an exercise in astrophysics, he sighed and said 'I really like making technos. But,' he shrugged and shook his head, 'Partnering Zumi... I ask you!'

I didn't know what to say. Though Tutor-Henny insists that we never complain, Zumi is hard to get along with, and she's sooo competitive. The only way I cope is by trying not to show how angry she makes me. She and Trist really clash. Sometimes, like when she's that bit slower to solve a problem, he'll tell her she's stupid. And once, in an exercise on Molecular Physics, he lashed out at her avatar. As any attempt to use physical force is unforgivable, their tutors usually keep them apart.

What will it feel like being with all four Hatchlings? Will Trist get angry if I pay more attention to Jafet? What if it's the other way around? How will Zumi behave when she's with both mascs? What will it be like when all four of us are expected to work together? What is even more worrying – how will I cope without Tutor-Henny beside me?

***

Now Jafet's avatar appears in my Cell. If Zumi's avatar has curly coal-black hair, smooth dark skin and eyes, high cheekbones, slender hips and long strong legs, my avatar's face is equally perfect. She has a long strong body, yellow curls, blue eyes and pink skin. Jafet's avatar is a head taller, with a shock of fair hair, blue eyes the exact shade of the sky above that lovely valley, a square chin, a sturdy chest and magnificent biceps and quads. 'Hiya, Pya, Zumi!' He holds out his arms and spins. 'Well…What do you think?'

'Hiya, Jafet,' I say, hoping my avatar still holds up. One time when Trist and I were working on a project in quantum physics, my avatar lost both arms. Though I pretended it didn't matter, tears dripped down my cheeks. It took ages for me to feel confident enough to work with him again.

'Well…What do you think?' he repeats, this time rather anxiously.

Zumi's avatar doesn't bother hiding her yawn.

Jafet ignores Zumi. 'Pya…' he insists. 'Tell me what you think.'

'Brilliant,' I cry, though I can't see any difference. Jafet's avatars always look wonderful.

'Your avatars are so successful,' he insists, his smile almost blindingly white. 'I've always admired them tremendously. They're so creative, they remind me of some seventh and

9

eighth millennia artwork...'

He rattles on. Zumi's avatar examines her perfect oval fingernails. I can't help smiling. Jafet always makes me feel good. I just wish... well, sometime I wish his praise wasn't so over the top. More to the point, I wish he'd shut up. If only he didn't sound like a Universal-Dictionary. Eventually, he stops talking long enough to look puzzled. 'What is presently happening? No tutors and all four avatars in the Cells together. I have never previously been joined by more than one Hatchling.'

'Me neither,' I tell him. 'Isn't Trist supposed to be here?'

At this, another masc, as tall and handsome and muscular as Jafet, only with brown skin, black eyes, an equally perfect torso and limbs, plus a shock of curly black hair, slides in from behind.

'Hi Trist,' we call. But my Cell is too small. From above, we four must resemble a Saturn air-octopus, all knotted heads, bodies, arms and legs.

Trist is first to quarter-size. He cartwheels and walks back on his hands. Jafet quarter-sizes too, and tries to top Trist with a triple somersault. Trist back-flips and ends up beside me. I pretend this is no big deal. How come I can never get my avatar to flip-flop like theirs?

Finally Zumi and I quarter-size. Now we can fit into a small space, everyone squats a hand-span above the floor.

Zumi coughs impatiently. 'Time wasted is time lost!'

We're so sick of our Tutor-Holos saying this, Trist sits on her head. While she tries to wriggle out from under, I can't help giggling. You wouldn't believe how often I've wanted to do just that.

ComCen buts in mind-saying, 'First exercise will begin NOW!'

3

Avatars

There's the usual dizzy making transition that happens when our avatars move to a different location. Now we're in an entirely new holo; a walking track in a tropical rain-forest. 'As you proceed,' *ComCen* instructs, 'note the various ferns, grasses, orchids and bracken.'

This rain-forest is large, wet and dense with trees and shrubbery. Our track merges in and out of a hollow which smells of decaying vegetation and soft damp earth. This almost, if not quite, overlays my Cell's usual metallic odour. Everything here is intensely green and eye-blindingly colourful. Outsized rainbow parrots squawk and clatter from trees dripping with fruit. Luminescent monarch butterflies flutter overhead, and every leaf hides a multitude of insects and grubs.

Yet there are hints that this isn't real. My feet hover just above the winding track and when I touch a tree-trunk, my hand slides right through it.

This track finally leads us to a lake flanked by large stones. 'Waterbend Lake,' *ComCen* tells us. 'This is your first session in Social Interaction. It will take place in Ancient Times. Your instructions are to set aside individual conflicts and cooperate as a team.'

***

Maybe you're wondering what *ComCen* is? Is She more than a complex, intricate computer? Sometimes I picture her as a fem with kind brown eyes, a perfect oval face, soft full lips and brown flowing hair. Other times, such as when *She's* telling me what to do and there's no answering back, I see her as detached as outer space, a mere shadow flickering against a wall. Occasionally, I visualise a wispy cloud that lights up whenever She speaks. Whatever... I always think of *ComCen* as *She*.

She, or the part of *ComCen* I call Tutor-Henny, is always with me. One of my first memories is chucking my kuddly and it flying right through her. That was when I first understood that Tutor-Henny wasn't real, that she was just a holo. When I was little, I threw lots of tantrums to try and get my own way. I was never punished. Rather, she would merely insist that I make a bigger effort to complete whatever project we were working on. Maybe if I had someone real to argue with, someone that's not just a giant computer, someone who could sometimes make a mistake, I might be less stubborn. As it is, these failures always leave me angry and frustrated.

***

Our avatars stride above that lushly green garden. More colourful birds and butterflies flutter overhead. In Waterbend

Lake, tiny fish dart about in the shallows. Frogs croak. Cicadas trill. No one speaks. We're too busy taking everything in.

I watch the others. No one says much. What can we say? We all know this is only a recreation of some place in the very distant past that was totally destroyed and can never be recovered. It's lovely to be here, but it also makes me sad. Tears drip down my real face. I wipe them away.

What else can I tell you about the others? Only that Jafet gets on well with everyone. Maybe too well. For example if I was to say 'Avatars are real', I suspect he wouldn't argue, rather he'd try to explain how this couldn't be true. He'll do just about anything to avoid an argument. Conflict makes him uncomfortable.

Trist is great with all technology and getting his avatars to do back-flips and cartwheel. But he also enjoys a fight. This mostly consists of goading us fems until we yell back. Me, he teases a little. Zumi a lot. Not that she doesn't deserve it. She's so hard to get along with. But does he know that she builds stunning sculptures? Is he aware that I program my own plasto-steel synth? Even if he is, he'll never acknowledge that we fems might have something he'd enjoy knowing more about.

However, Zumi is my biggest problem, as she's my major work-partner. She'll say anything that pops into her mind, no matter how competitive or nasty. Our last assignment — we were working on **coelacanths** — a dust particle floated around my Cell, and my real body sneezed and blinked out her holo. 'Honestly Pya,' she shouted. 'All that work gone to waste. Wait'll I tell Tutor-Hecate what a fool you are...'

She went on and on, until I yelled back, 'Wasn't my fault. I didn't know I was going to sneeze...'

I wasn't allowed to finish...

'...you're always messing things up. No wonder Tutor-Hecate told me Tutor-Henny says you're hard to control...'

'Tutor-Henny says what?' My heart quickened. What is she saying about me? Before I could retort, communication between us was cut off. But knowing how horrid Zumi can be makes my blood boil.

Presently, I peer into Waterbend Lake. A girl with long blonde hair and a strong pink body stares back at me. I lean forward to inspect her. My avatar is holding up just fine. I sit back to watch the mascs leap from rock to rock. It's then an idea hits me – one so strange, I can hardly believe it popped into my mind. I whisper to Zumi so the mascs won't hear, 'I've had an idea...What if we were to see our real bodies?'

'Huh?' Zumi reacts as if I've just lost my head, this being about the worst thing that can happen, even worse than losing both arms, as it's so confusing for the recipient. 'Why would you want to do that?'

'I know our actual bodies look almost the same. Tutor-Henny insists that it's hard to tell us apart.'

'Hmmph.' Zumi hates me talking like this. 'Honestly Pya. That's why we use avatars. They're to protect us and make us look better.'

'We don't even know for sure what our avatars are supposed to look like. What if they're wrong? Anyway, we're so busy working, we never have fun.'

'No way,' she yells indignantly. 'Aren't Trist and Jafet having fun? Why would you want to risk your real body getting hurt?' The clear pool reflects her shudder. 'You know how fragile our bodies are.'

'I suppose so. Only...' even to me this sounds weird, 'sometimes I'd like to know what things really feel like...'

'Honestly Pya, sometimes I don't know what you're on

about. Give it up,' she whines and turns.'

I smile wryly and watch the mascs triple somersault into the pool. Eventually my avatar joins in. She dives into the water, swims down one end and back, floats effortlessly while watching a platypus build her nest inside a tunnel. Even though my body isn't actually here, I enjoy myself, though the water slides off me like there's a transparent wall between us.

What if I really was here?

'Listen Zumi…' I insist, even though if I keep on like this, she'll simply walk away. 'Wouldn't you like to be swimming for real?'

Zumi's avatar pouts. 'But we do everything this way. What if we were to hurt ourselves?'

'Of course.' Tutor-Henny always claims that I'm too persistent. 'I'm just being stupid. Still,' I muse. 'We've done all this before. I wouldn't mind something different even if it does hurt a bit. I just want to know what things feel like...'

The pool suddenly vanishes.

Zumi and I spring to our feet.

ComCen is moving us to a different location. What was a lushly green tropical garden morphs into a concrete funfair. What were trees turn into giant whirly-bird hair-raising rides. Next, our four avatars are standing at the entrance of a giant funfair.

I point. 'What does that sign mean?'

'Ancient Times.' Jafet gestures at another. 'That says 'Cave of the Unknowns.'

'What's that?' Zumi asks.

'Maybe more about *The Great Disaster*?' Trist suggests.

Everyone sighs. Not again... not again...

'Anyway,' Jafet says in this prissy voice. 'We'd never let

another Disaster happen. And you Pya, would be additionally cautious, wouldn't you.'

Zumi's avatar goes scarlet. 'What makes you think it'd be up to Pya, huh?'

I don't say anything. I know she's angling for a fight. Jafet's avatar copes by running ahead. Trist's avatar continues practising back-flips. He cartwheels on until he lands beside Jafet and asks, 'How come you can read those signs?'

'*ComCen* filled my brain with the right words. This language was spoken on Terra, many millennia ago. But this is only one. Back then people spoke lots of different languages. At last count there were over three thousand, including various dialects...'

He would have gone on like this forever except Zumi's avatar snorts, 'What if they couldn't understand each other? What a mess that'd be.'

I agree. But even if we do know what the other Hatchlings say, I don't see us as any better.

Jafet never takes offence. Always the peacemaker, his avatar merely smiles. 'It certainly was. Sometimes these led to conflicts which became extremely serious once they developed nuclear technology...'

ComCen buts in with, 'Shortly, everything will be explained.'

Trist's avatar runs through the entrance. 'Let's explore,' he calls. 'Okay?'

'Okay, okay.' A funfair is something we can share. Aren't we supposed to be working together?

Our avatars follow Trist into a dark tunnel. As we enter we pass a sign reading: Cave of Terrors. Inside, all I see are rough stone walls and a roof that fades into darkness. Two metal rails run along the floor. A little further, they turn left. In the opposite direction, a small enclosed engine with a smokestack breathing steam trundles towards us pulling two open cabins. 'An ancient train,' says Jafet. 'They used coal to fuel their engines...'

He's about to explain the mechanics, but Trist pushes him into the first cabin. Zumi and I slide into the second, and the engine sets off. It takes us past a Martian snake. When that snake uncoils and darts towards us, Zumi and I clutch each other and squeal. Martian snakes don't have to bite as their touch is lethal. But we aren't seriously frightened. We know these creatures are only holos that can't hurt us.

The next holo is a fem. But this is no ordinary fem. As wide as she is tall, she towers above us. Her pointy teeth are covered in steel, she wears a boar's head tattoo on her right shoulder and its tusks run down one arm. But it's her eyes that make me squirm. Set inside heavy brows and wide cheekbones, they make me shudder

Towards the end of our ride, another creature sends even more tremors down my spine. It's a Betelguex Shape-Shifter, the monster Jafet and I have often spoken about. Scary it certainly is, but you can't help admiring the way it morphs from a multi-snake-tongued lizard, to a cave-tiger teeth dripping blood, then a giant tiger, a giant bat and finally to shadow that can't be caught. Of course this is why the Shape-Shifter is acknowledged as the most terrifying creature in the universe.

Though these are only holos, when the cart trundles through a door and back outside, I breathe a sigh of relief. 'Great ride,' Trist yells. 'Let's try another.'

4

Entering the City

Our avatars head to Slide Forever and climb on. First me. Then Jafet. Then Trist. Zumi comes last. We slide down extra fast in a bump-free ride. Not that our avatar bottoms ever make real contact. Nor do our avatar hands really grip this slide's sides.

We rush down... down...taking each new curve faster than the last, building up more and more speed. This ride isn't called Slide Forever for nothing.

What if it never stops?

What if it goes on forever?

I break into a cold sweat. Tell myself not to panic. None of this is really exists. This is merely an extended holo. Nothing can happen. Avatars can never be injured. Down... down we rush, the wind pushing my hair into my face so I can hardly see. One more curve before hitting bottom...

Oh no! People... milling about... right in front... I'm about to plunge right into them.

But this is only Virtual. If Slide Forever was real, my avatar is about to get terribly hurt...

I hit a fat masc, push right through him and land with a thump on the ground.

Ouch!

That really hurt!

Back in my Cell, I sit there, stunned.

I feel as if I've really landed on extra hard ground... that it was not my avatar a hand-span above that ground, but that it was me-

I feel as if someone punched out all my air.

I'm sure my coccyx is covered in black and blue welts.

This is seriously weird. This is how my real body would feel if it landed on a hard surface.

But isn't this only a holo? Aren't I working through my avatar? No wonder Tutor-Henny accuses me of too much imagination. Could this be *ComCen*'s way of helping our avatars experience a little more?

Nothing else makes sense.

I move my avatar onto a nearby bench. My body is still in my Cell. So why is my heart ready to jump out of my chest? Why do I feel so battered and bruised?

Who are these people?

Why are they here?

My heart won't stop thudding. My stomach feels weak. Sweat trickles down my back.

Of course this is only a holo... only make-believe... only pretend.

Then why does it feel so dangerous?

I concentrate on that fat masc's thick crop of grey hair, red nose and cheeks. His belly seems as large as my sleeping pod. His companion-fem has fine wrinkly skin, white hair caught in a bun, and uses a walking stick. I suspect that this couple is what Tutor-Henny describes as 'old'. Yet in a way, the fem's worn soft cheeks and slow careful manner remind me of her.

Why did Tutor-Henny decide to leave just when I need her? My hands won't stop shaking. In just a few seconds, my whole world has turned upside down. What makes things worse is that I can tell nothing similar happened to the others.

Zumi slides onto my bench. She's smiling. Of course she's smiling. She hasn't experienced anything unusual. My avatar's fall... the one I thought my body suffered... surely it was only my imagination. Tutor-Henny always says my over-active mind will get me into trouble. So I can't say anything to the others because they will only laugh. But I feel as if I've been dragged through a tunnel backwards. I feel as though there's a black hole under me, and that if I don't watch out, that I'll fall through...

Zumi whispers, 'Isn't this amazing? I'd like it heaps higher and faster. Pya, you're such a scaredy cat. Bet you were terrified.'

'Course I wasn't,' I whisper indignantly, though I'm sure nothing unusual happened to her. Why are we whispering? Ancient Times is merely an extended holo. Those people are only holos. No way can they hear what we're saying.

Now Zumi stops still long enough to study the old masc and fem. Her mouth twists with disgust. 'Ugh! So ugly and stupid.'

'How do you know they're stupid?'

'Well, they wouldn't look like that if they weren't stupid, would they. Where are their avatars?'

'These are what real humans truly look like,' I tell her.

'They're old. Maybe you haven't seen holos of old mascs and fems before.'

Zumi frowns. 'What exactly is old?'

'*ComCen* is old.'

She glances away. '*ComCen* doesn't look old.'

'We don't know what *ComCen* looks like,' I remind her. 'Only what *ComCen* sounds like.'

'So how come *She* sounds like a fem?'

'Maybe sometimes *She's* a masc,' I muse.

'Maybe *She* is.' Zumi pauses to think this over. 'At least we know what our tutor-holos look like.'

I bite my lip. 'Not really.' I manage to stay calm. 'We only know what their avatars look like. Maybe they don't look like anything. Even if we're almost identical, I don't know what your real body looks like except for what I see when I look down at myself.'

She wrinkles her nose and turns away. 'I still think those primitives are ugly.'

As there's no way to convince her otherwise, I look for the others. Jafet is watching a small boy lick a fluffy white substance on a yellow stick. I glimpse Trist cart-wheeling towards us. 'Let's check out more rides,' he calls.

I can tell nothing unusual happened to those mascs.

Only to me.

But there's no time to brood on this as Zumi and I set off after Jafet. Trist attaches himself to a masc and a fem with three hatchlings. *ComCen* mind-says, 'This is a Family. Back in the mid twenty-first century, many humans lived in small groups which often contained a Mother, a Father and one or more Hatchlings.'

ComCen continues to explain that this Family's masc is called Charlie and their fem, Rio. 'These Hatchlings are twins.

They were hatched exactly the same day and time as you, only many, many thousands of years in the past.'

Both youngsters have thick dark-brown hair, almond-shaped brown eyes, small turned up noses, wide pink mouths and smooth round faces. Their bodies and limbs are lean and strong. Perhaps their major difference is the fem's longer hair and teeth surrounded by a clear band.

I turn my attention to the newest Hatchling. I can't tell whether it's a fem or a masc as most is hidden under a cover. It cries so loudly we have to place our hands over our ears to drown out the noise. No one else seems to care. The hatchling gives one more wail, places a thumb inside its mouth and falls asleep.

'The adult masc and fem are a Mother and Father,' Jafet explains.

Those adults are tall. Their arms and legs are long and sturdy, their faces slightly creased. When I point this out, Jafet says, 'Those lines are called wrinkles. Most adults have them.'

'What is the adults' specific task?' I ask Jafet.

'Not sure,' he admits. 'But most Families seem to have at least one Mother, sometimes even a Mother and a Father...'

'I know why,' Trist buts in. We wait for him to back-flip. 'The Mother and Father have this weird way of making Hatchlings. I can tell you how, only it'll make your real bodies want to throw up.'

We watch Rio talk with Mother. Then she runs to an outdoor room displaying small furry objects. She hands over a slip of paper to a fem standing behind the stall. For this she is given a small fluffy object that she places inside the youngest Hatchling's cart.

Mother smiles. Father nods. The hatchling sleeps. Charlie kicks the dusty track. 'He's bored,' Trist remarks. 'Should be with other mascs.'

'Only grown ancients.' Jafet shakes his head. 'No others his age must be frustrating.'

'What about the fem?' I but in.

'Huh?' Trist dismisses this. 'Not the same.'

'Course not,' Jafet interjects. 'Interaction between fem and masc is never entirely successful.'

Zumi frowns. 'What's wrong with them working together?'

Jafet pretends not to hear. Trist completes a cartwheel. We follow the Family, our feet hovering just above the ground, towards a blue metallic chariot on four wheels. The Family climb inside. Our avatars leap onto the roof. We glimpse an entrance to another ride.

'What does it say?' Zumi asks Jafet.

'Dinosaur Times.'

'Wonder where it leads,' I muse.

'You're such an idiot,' Zumi yells. 'Just what it says.'

I bite my lip and pretend not to hear. The mascs are only interested in the ancient car which Trist tells us runs on fossil fuel.

'So wasteful,' says Jafet, 'when there are no fossil fuels or minerals left on Terra or the moon. They tried nuclear energy, but there were so many accidents in the end they resorted to wind-farms, solar and sea-tide, though there was never enough to power to go around, this leading to trade wars culminating in *The Great Disaster*,...'

Only the chariot starting up stops Jafet in midsentence. We examine the chariot's structure, engine and underside. Eventually we come to a road lined with buildings. Halfway down, the chariot stops. 'This is where this Family resides,' *ComCen* informs us.

We're in front of a single storey concrete building with a

pitched roof much like holos I've seen of ninth millennium houses on Mars. 'What do they do with so much space?' Trist asks.

ComCen says, 'There's a Cell for a viewing machine, a Cell to dispense food and liquid, and a personal hygiene Cell that deposits fresh water.'

'How much fresh water?' I ask.

'As much as they want,' *ComCen* replies.

Our eyes widen. We can't believe that such extravagance has ever existed. Water is the most precious commodity in our galaxy.

'And,' *ComCen* adds, 'in this Family, all Hatchlings have a separate sleeping cell.'

'No wonder we ran out of resources,' I say indignantly. By now I've dismissed what happened on Slide Forever. Doesn't Tutor-Henny insist that I'm the victim of my own imagination? The others admire the garden as it's always a pleasure to enter a holo with this many flowers. The Family climb out of the chariot and walk down a path. 'Are we going inside?' Zumi asks Jafet.

He heads towards the front door. 'I imagine that's *ComCen*'s intention...'

Seems *ComCen* has other ideas. Next, I'm back in my Cell with Tutor-Henny handing me a drink-tube. She massages the back of my head where my knowledge button sits. I'm stiff from sitting in my chair-pod too long. My bottom feels sore and bruised. Henny says, 'Your body needs nourishment. This project will continue tomorrow.'

I lean back in my chair. Right now I'm too tired to ask why things went wrong on Slide Forever. I sleep and sleep. And while I sleep, I dream…

'So…' First Voice ruminates. 'You intend catapulting them right in? Their bodies are small and weak. What if they won't stand up to the strain?'

'Then they will be deemed a failure,' says another voice.

A shiver runs down my spine. This voice is as cold and empty as space.

'A failure!' First Voice sighs. 'After we have spent so much time and effort on their growth and development. What will happen to them then?'

'Then…' Second Voice is quite matter-of-fact. 'Then we start all over again…'

My heart gives a sickening jolt. In my dream I strain to hear more. But there is nothing… nothing…

I stay awake a long time puzzling over this. Was it a dream or did I really hear voices discussing what might happen if we are 'deemed a failure'?

Eventually I fall asleep, and once again I dream. But this dream is unbelievably scary. In it, I'm hurtling into an unknown galaxy where a billion suns almost blind me with their awesome luminosity. Now I'm falling… plummeting through space until I come to an extra bright sun orbited by ten planets.

The first planet is only lifeless rock that splits so often, the surface quivers in a permanent earthquake. I skirt around it and keep moving, tumbling past four more planets until I finally land on the sixth.

I'm standing in a desert of yellow sand and brown hills. A giant orange sun dips below the horizon. Nothing moves. Nothing grows. Only endless dunes stretching as far as the eye can see. A low wind builds up speed and whips around me. Dust-devils spiral. My skin prickles. My pulse throbs. As I stand there trembling, I'm desperate to escape. Somehow I know something dreadful is about to happen ... something mind-blowing and horrible...

5

Reality

I start up. It takes me a long moment to realise that I'm still in my Cell, and Tutor-Henny is bending over me. I breathe a huge sigh of relief. Those were only dreams. Only nightmares.

I'm given a searching glance, but Tutor-Henny asks no questions. Instead she helps me use my toilet-pod and swallow two food-tubes that she assures me contain enough protein, fibre, minerals, vitamins and calories to make me feel better.

Shortly, I do.

Whenever I enter my avatar, my real body takes ages to recover. Not that Tutor-Henny ever explains why this happens. Also, I'm, aware of other issues. Sooner or later as we keep growing we're going to need much bigger Cells and longer sleep-pods. I can't imagine being grown-up and still living in this tiny space. But there's always the hope that if *ComCen* moves me to a bigger Cell, I'll get a chance to see what's outside Circle 3, Great Southern Continent, Terra. Sometimes I wonder why my Cell has to be this small. If Tutor-Henny is right, and we are the only Hatchlings left on Terra, how come we can't have more space?

Too many unanswered questions. Yet whenever I ask Tutor-Henny, all she'll ever say is, 'All in good time.'

Each time I persist with 'But what is good time?' Tutor-Henny's eyes turn frosty grey. 'I keep telling you not to be so impatient. You must wait for *ComCen*'s instructions.' I sigh and nod. Maybe things would be easier if *ComCen* wasn't just a disembodied mind-voice and I could argue back. I recall our last assignment. All that space those ancients had! I'm totally envious. Other things bother me, too. Why did Rio give the manikin to the younger Hatchling? Why was Charlie bored? But my major questions are: Why did Tutor-Henny desert me when I most needed her? Why was my avatar the only one to experience pain?

Sunk in thought, when my tutor asks, 'Pya, tell me what's on your mind...' I reply, 'I'm just tired.'

Doesn't she always know what I'm thinking? Doesn't *ComCen* monitor all my thoughts and emotions? So instead of asking why I was singled out in this curious way, I say sulkily, 'Why are you interested?'

Her eyes turn their usual soft brown. '*ComCen* is concerned that all the Hatchlings are doing well.'

'Can't you tell?'

Tutor-Henny downsizes so the top of her head only reaches my waist. 'We know if your blood sugar levels are low, and we can regulate your pulse and hormone levels.' Her smile never wavers. 'But sometimes it is hard to know how lively your mood might be.' She gazes at my food-drink-tubes as if the answer might lie there. 'Perhaps you are receiving too many minerals. Maybe not enough. Or not exercising enough.'

The back of my chair lowers and she cries, 'Time wasted is time lost. A lesson must always be followed by meditation-time.'

I sigh loudly. But Tutor-Henny always makes it clear that I can never interfere with meditation-time as this is supposed to keep my brain and body alert.

She says, 'Repeat your visualisation.'

I picture myself approaching that village in the lovely green valley. Only this time there's no moving into a dark future. One house is particularly inviting. I head inside past a room with comfortable sitting pods, up a flight of stairs and down the passage to a room lined with holos of pleasant landscapes. A large white sleeping pod is in the centre of the room. Meanwhile Tutor-Henny's hands move up and down my body massaging away any tension and pain. Gradually, gradually as I slide under the covers, my body relaxes...

Next, I'm shaken awake. Tutor-Henny says, 'While you slept, *ComCen* filled your knowledge button with language to cope with Ancient Times. Now the team will have no difficulty in naming what they come across.'

There's the usual dizzy-making transition when I'm returned to my avatar.

Now I'm standing by the entrance of Ancient Times. The other four are here too.

'Hurry up, Pya,' Trist calls impatiently.

'What's happening?'

'*ComCen* wants us to find out more about that Twenty-First Century Family.'

'Great!' I'm relieved not to be returned to Slide Forever.

'Just look at that!' Trist cries in open admiration. A roofless red vehicle heads our way. It has silvery hubcaps.

Hubcaps: the central and protective part of a wheel.

Now everything I see has its correct name and usage.

Our avatars climb into the car. We travel along a curving road until we come to the outskirts of a large city. It is the same City we visited before but this time everything is different. Buildings are either completely destroyed or badly damaged. Street lights are smashed, walls covered in graffiti, shop-fronts boarded over, gutters filled with rubbish. No people. Not anywhere. We're appalled at so much destruction.

'What's been happening here?' Zumi asks in a small voice.

ComCen doesn't answer. How come? *She* always answers our questions. A shiver runs down my spine. Everything here feels terribly wrong. Finally we come to the same house we'd visited before, only the front looks as if a bomb glanced off it, though the back is still intact. Our car stops. We climb out and walk inside. The front rooms are badly damaged, but we walk into a door that leads into the kitchen. As we come in, the young masc called Charlie is saying 'Can't wait to be old enough.'

Mother sighs. 'Ordinary folk haven't a chance. Street gangs are far too powerful.'

'Why are they called Snouts?' Rio asks.

'They wear pig masks,' says Father, 'to make themselves even more frightening than they already are.'

We listen. Since our last visit there's been a civil war. Once the worst of the bombing was over, the City was taken over by a gang called 'Snouts'. Neither the police nor the army are strong enough to control them.

I turn my attention to the older people. Father must be

at least quadruple my height, his eyes and hair as dark as the twins, only his face is slightly crooked, as if one side has slipped away from the other. Mother is shorter than Father. She has slanted dark eyes, pink cheeks, a wide mouth with full lips, and a soft round body like Tutor-Henny. As I watch her hug Rio, I have a strange sense of loss.

Father leaves. 'He's gone to look for food,' Mother tells her Hatchlings. As she places the Hatchling she calls 'Emma' in her sleeping pod, Zumi's avatar finds a crust of bread. She places it in her mouth. Chews and swallows.

Our jaws drop. Then we all talk at once: 'Did you really eat that...?'

'How is this possible-?'

'What does it taste like-?'

'Terrific-' A crumb sticks in Zumi-avatar's throat. She nearly chokes. 'Reckon you're too scared to try.'

'Yah!' Trist's avatar sneers. 'Bet your avatar isn't really eating.'

'Sure is.' Her avatar crams another piece into her mouth. 'It's delicious.'

I'm truly bewildered. 'Avatars are only Virtual. They're not Actual. So how come Zumi is eating real food?'

She points to another crust. 'Try some.'

Trist's avatar cartwheels to the table and takes a piece. I watch this food enter his mouth. I watch him chew. He coughs and chokes.

'What's it like?'

He swallows before saying, 'Like a red, brown and yellow food-tube all mixed together. Only the texture is rough. Hard to swallow'

I pop the last morsel into my mouth. Rub my tongue over it. Trist was right. The texture is coarse and crunchy. A crumb

31

hits the back of my throat. My eyes water. I'm too busy trying to catch my breath to ask how come our avatars can feel, taste and swallow?

Mother picks up the empty plate. 'Where's the rest of the bread?'

Rio and Charlie are too busy arguing to answer. Mother sighs. We have taken their breakfast. The Family don't have enough to eat. From everything we hear, it seems gangs have stolen most of the City's food and fuel.

Breakfast over the older Hatchlings continue to bicker over two tablets. One is apparently newer. Both want it. Charlie wins through his superior physical strength. Rio sulks. Finally, she takes the lesser and wanders outside to a garden surrounded by a wall topped with broken glass. Mother watches her through a window. 'Rio, if you hear anything unusual, you're to come straight inside.'

Rio's response is to climb into a small house built into a tree-trunk. We follow. This house is small. Just like Cell Q3. In it, I feel very much at home. Rio browses files with names like 'Bunny', and 'Ms. Sophisticate'. I read over her shoulder. She sighs. I understand her sigh. Seems we're all unhappy with the way we look.

Midday, she runs back into the house. We follow. The next meal is something Charlie calls 'noodles'. Though our avatars taste a few, this time we're careful to leave most untouched. The texture is slippery. There's less danger of choking.

'Like yellow and white food-tubes with a slightly chewier texture,' Jafet decides.

After lunch, the Mother says, 'Rio, clear the table, will you?'

'Why?' she whines. 'It's Charlie's turn.'

Mother sighs. 'Must you always argue?'

Rio sulks but does as she's told only interrupting this

ctivity to communicate on her primitive wrist-phone with someone called Gena.

I listen in. First they mention how much they miss each other. They go on to talk about their Learning Cell. Rio says, '...an' she said Frankel was awful to Amy, so I said it serves Amy right for being such a know-it-all, and then she hung up on me...'

Most of their conversation is about friends, clothes, synth and mascs. Though many of their learning exercises are completed on these antique tablets, they must also attend a vast Cell called school. What I hear is how the City is too dangerous for Father to return to his place of work or for the twins to leave the house. Rio says, 'It's so boring here and Charlie argues about everything. Least we can talk to each other. Mum says we're lucky these work but she doesn't think that'll last.'

'Those two are so immature,' Zumi's avatar says in disgust. 'Don't they ever talk about important things?'

'Like what?'

'Well...' She thinks. 'Like what they learn?'

'Why? We don't.'

'Course we do,' she says indignantly.

'We talk about Trist, Jafet, avatars, holos, synth and *ComCen*. In their talk, that's boys, lessons, music and school, isn't it?'

'Not the same thing,' she mutters.

Course it is. But I'm sick of arguing. Why must she always disagree with everything I say?

Curious about how this Family lives, we peer into cupboards, behind chairs and under carpets. We watch them come and go until bedtime.

But all this time *ComCen* remains silent. Why? Where are

our tutor-holos? Isn't it time we were returned to our Cells?

We wait and wait.

But all that happens is that the light in this room changes.

It's suddenly very bright.

Very hard.

Very harsh.

So much light makes my eyes water, and my mouth go dry.

It sends my heart into my mouth.

What can it mean?

PART 2

ACTUALITY

6

Stuck!

We wait and wait. This Cell is so large and so bright, my eyes won't stop watering. The noise level has increased. It makes my ears ring. My mouth is dry. My belly hurts. So does my head. My body is stiff and sore. I think I might throw up. Am I getting The Great Plague? If so I'll die. But I don't want to die... I just want to go back to Cell Q3 and hear Tutor-Henny say, 'Time wasted is time lost.'

We wait and wait. Nothing happens. Well, nothing except for Zumi's avatar moaning, 'Why doesn't Tutor-Hecate take me home?'

In the end Trist's avatar gets so fed up, he yells, 'Zumi, we all want to go home. If you don't shut up I'll... I'll...' He stops as he remembers what happened last time he hit her avatar.

We squat in a corner of this large Cell and hang around

for what seems like three sleeps. We doze and wake up long enough to complain to each other how bad we feel. Finally the Father turns up carrying two small parcels. By then my real throat is too dry to talk. My real belly is sore. The others feel the same.

'These sensations are very unpleasant,' Jafet complains. 'Pya, do you have any idea of why is this happening?'

'No,' I manage through cracked lips. Can this be what true hunger and thirst feels like?

'So why doesn't *ComCen* bring us back?' Jafet whispers.

But *ComCen* remains silent. *She* sends no instructions. Not even a hint about when our avatars will close down and we'll be taken back to our Cells.

Something is seriously wrong. The others don't bother hiding how frightened they are. As the hours drag on, my belly hurts even more. The pain is only eased by curling into a ball. I keep on wondering if we've caught The Great Plague? Are the others thinking the same? If so, we'll die, we'll surely die...

I try to concentrate on the Family. The Father has come home looking pleased. Though there are terrible food shortages, he's found a small bunch of carrots and a few potatoes. I slide over and touch a potato. My finger comes away covered in dirt.

My avatar never makes actual contact.

So how come my finger is dirty?

My mind goes blank.

The Mother cuts the potatoes and cooks them in oil. The smell makes my real mouth water. It must be happening to the others too, because Trist's avatar crawls up beside the Mother and steals a slice.

'Scrumptious.' He crams another slice into his mouth. We

watch him wide-eyed. Then we three do the same. We chew and swallow very slowly. The food disappears. Now we feel slightly better. But this leads to many questions. How come this is happening? How come our avatars can pick up food and then our real bodies taste, chew and swallow? I can only think that somehow our *real* and *virtual* bodies have melded.

But this isn't possible...

Or is it?

Charlie wanders in and stands beside me. I'm too bewildered to be scared. Anyway, I know he can't see me. He asks, 'Mum, what's to eat?'

Mother is scrubbing and cutting up carrots. 'Bread. Chips. Carrots.'

'Chips?' Charlie looks around the kitchen. 'Where?'

'On the table behind you.'

He sees an empty plate. 'No, they aren't.'

Mother looks at the plate and cries, 'Charlie, how could you?'

Charlie stares at her, bewildered. 'Could I what?'

'Eat all those chips. And this morning, you ate all the toast.'

'But I didn't,' he protests.

Rio and Father wander into the kitchen. 'Charlie ate all the chips,' Mother says crossly. 'Now there's nothing left.'

'Oh Charlie!' Father sounds tired. 'It took me all day to find those potatoes.'

Charlie is so upset, he chokes up. 'But I didn't eat them. I didn't...'

Father doesn't believe him. Our avatars use the ensuing row to taste their bread. The texture is interesting. Soft and chewy. This time I'm careful to eat v-e-r-y slowly. I take a carrot. This is harder. I have to chew and chew before I dare swallow. It's good, though. Fresh. Crunchy. I don't stop to wonder how come I can taste and feel. I'm far too hungry. Anyway, I calm down by telling myself this is all to do with this new exercise. Just a matter of waiting for Tutor-Henny to explain it all. I'm sure this is part of this latest assignment. I just wish I knew why it's taking so long to complete, and why it's so hard.

Father says, 'I know growing boys use lots of energy. But why keep denying it?'

'But I didn't steal those chips,' Charlie just about shrieks.

Mother now sees that the rest of the food has disappeared. She wails, 'And he took those carrots…'

Charlie storms out, slamming the door behind him.

Rio looks smug. 'He's such a jerk!'

Mother smiles wryly. 'Don't call your brother names.' But her tone hints she's says this far too often.

We watch and listen. The longer we stay, the less impressed we are. 'Those Hatchlings are always squabbling,' Zumi coolly observes. 'Wonder why they stay together? I wouldn't.'

I'm not so sure. Watching Mother cuddle Emma-Hatchling leaves a hollow in my chest. I wish I could also live in the twenty-first century with a Mother, Father and an Emma. Anyway, this assignment seems to be going on forever. Why we aren't being returned to our Cells? Where is Tutor-Henny? Why doesn't *ComCen* talk to us? Why has *She* left us here? What are we supposed to be doing?

What is going on?

'Beans. All we have left.' Mother holds out a can. 'But I don't know what we'll eat tomorrow.'

The beans are little and white and sit in a runny red sauce. The Family eat in silence. The food quickly disappears.

'I'm still hungry,' Rio moans. Both Mother and Father look sad.

I wonder how Charlie feels? He's eaten even less.

But I can't be worried about him. All I want is to be back in my Cell with Tutor-Henny looking after me singing Time Wasted is Time Lost.

Where is *she*?

What is going on?

Why is this happening?

Tutor-Henny where are you?

7

Actuality is Scary

Their meal over, Mother dips their dishes in enough water to last us Hatchlings a week. I still can't believe how wasteful these ancients are. They spend the rest of the evening in front of a Viewing Machine that keeps cutting out. So do their lamps. 'Street gangs raid electricity supplies,' Father wearily explains. When the power finally fails, the Family goes to bed.

We Hatchlings are also very tired. But *ComCen* seems to have forgotten us. How much longer does She intend leaving us here?

Charlie uses a torch to light the stairs, and we follow him and Rio. Halfway up he turns it off so he can trip her. She recovers just in time to yell, 'Jerk!'

'Pig,' he calls back. 'Bet you stole that food.'

She doesn't bother answering. In her own Cell, which is

large enough to take ten of our real bodies, by the flickering light of another torch, she removes her street clothes, pulls on different attire and climbs into her sleep-pod. Meanwhile Zumi and I go through her wardrobe. Zumi's avatar pulls out some pants. 'Too long,' I tell her and hand over a lacy top. 'Think my avatar would wear this top with those pants.'

'Jeans,' Zumi corrects me. 'Don't you know these are called jeans? Weren't you given language like the rest of us?'

I start to say something nasty back. But why bother? She'll only think of something worse. While we sift through Rio's clothes, Jafet and Trist explore her desk. Jafet's very excited to find another, and even more primitive tablet. 'Finding these fossils in one place is extraordinary, how rewarding it is to be back in this millennium...'

He's cut off by Trist holding up a box filled with paper. 'What's this for?'

'Writing?' I suggest.

'Impossible to write on anything this soft,' Jafet points out. 'Too absorbent.'

'Maybe they use it to mop up liquid?' I suggest.

Jafet says, 'If it is made of paper which comes from pulped woodchips, it must be used for writing.'

'Pya's right.' For once Zumi sides with me. 'They use these for mopping things up. Mascs are such idiots.'

Trist raises his fist. Only Jafet jumping between them prevents Zumi's avatar being fractured. My breath turns ragged. Without *ComCen* and our tutors, we're in enough trouble. Why can't those two ever stop? Eventually they calm down long enough to ignore each other.

Jafet reads Rio's personal thoughts. Zumi and I perch on the end of Rio's bed. She turns off her small bed-lamp and stares into the dark. I can hardly keep my eyes open. Tears roll down my cheeks. How come we we're still here? How come we aren't back in our Cells? Where is Henny?

Something else keeps troubling me. Back in my Cell, the only smell we knew was sharp and mechanical. Sometimes it tickled the back of my throat and made me cough and sneeze. But as it was always there, I usually managed to ignore it. So it is absence rather than presence that bothers me. 'Trist,' I wail. 'Why does everything smell different?'

Rio turns her bed-lamp back on and jumps to her knees. She holds out her sheet like a shield. 'I can hear you.' Her voice wobbles. 'Who are you? Why are you here?'

I start to spring onto her bed…only moving is too hard… my body is awkward… I can only move slowly… slowly… far too slowly…

I'm no longer in my avatar…

I'm in my real body…

…and I'm in this room.

Just like when I went down Slide Forever, Real and Virtual have fused into one!

It's happening again.

My mouth opens in a silent Help!!!!

What do I do now?

My heart beats so fast I think it might jump out of my chest.

Blood rushes to my head.

I'm chilled to the bone.

My lips go prickly. A swarm of tiny white lights drift across my field of vision and my body seems further away than it should be. The room starts to swim…

I'm about to faint…

Meanwhile Rio is yelling. 'Talk to me, will you?'

As I realise that she can see us… that we're no longer

invisible... I take a deep breath and try not to pass out.

Rio's still yelling, 'Talk to me, will you?'

The others can't answer either. They too shocked!

No speech! No movement.

Nothing!

Something extraordinary has happened. We're no longer in our avatars. We're not in our separate cells. We're really here... really in this room... our real bodies are in here with Rio.

Help! Tutor-Henny... *ComCen*... where are you?

'Talk, will you?' Rio shrieks.

No one is brave enough to say anything. Anyway, my mouth is too dry for anything to come out.

'Are you aliens?' Rio's eyes are wide with fright. 'Are you planning to kidnap me? Dad...' she starts to yell. Fortunately, Jafet pulls himself together and clamps his hand over her mouth. Rio's eyes bulge. She starts to cough and choke. I make a feeble attempt to pull his hand away.

Jafet finds his voice. 'Rio, p-promise you won't yell?'

She nods. Very slowly he takes his hand away. She rubs her lips. 'Who are you?' she whispers. 'Are you going to hurt me?'

We just stare. No one knows what to say.

Jafet finally finds his voice. 'Course not,' he says. 'Why would we harm you? Rest assured that this was never our intention. Why would we inflict any hurt on your person?'

'No.'

'Never.'

'Course not,' the rest of us cry.

We must look so scared, she finally believes us.

Tears roll down my cheeks. I try to wipe them away, but my movements are too slow. Even lifting a hand or an arm takes an immense effort. It's as if I'm moving in dense gravity...like at the bottom of a deep, deep sea... or been shifted to one of the planets circling X124DG.

What is happening to us?

My mouth curls in fright. I'm missing Tutor-Henny, my Cell, everything I'm so used to...

What are we doing here?

Why are we here?

Open mouthed, I stare at the others.

For a long, long moment, we just stare at each other, and then at our surroundings. Slowly, I become aware of the sheet under me. It's rough and cool. I'm no longer floating above it. Though the sensation is coarse and slightly prickly, it isn't as unpleasant as I might once have imagined.

There's a deadly silence as we take everything in. Then Jafet manages to croak, 'Can you really see us?'

'What do you think?' Rio must see how frightened we are because she cries, 'You just about choked me.'

'You… you can really, really see us?' Trist's voice quavers.

'I can hear you, too,' Rio says hotly. She shines her torch around the room. 'What are you doing in here? I'll bet it was you who stole that food.'

I giggle hysterically.

'And if it was you, that's so unfair,' she crossly cries. 'Making Charlie take the blame. And now you're going through my things. That's sooo rude.'

'What is rude?' Zumi is openly curious.

Rio glowers at her. 'Going through a person's stuff without permission.'

'Sorry,' Zumi mutters. I just stare. I'm sure this is the first time she has ever apologised to anyone. 'You see we didn't realise...' she's saying when Trist finally manages to climb onto the bed. 'Rio... can... can you really hear and see us?'

'Sure can.' Her voice still trembles. She swivels her bed-lamp onto Zumi, then the rest of us. 'You've got great big eyes, pale skins, pale hair, you're tiny and you're wearing skin-tight silver suits. She springs out of bed, runs to the door and turns on an overhead lamp.

The room is bathed in light.

Goggle-eyed, we stare at her. Then we turn to look at each other.

I'm rigid with shock. For the first time ever, we can see each other. We know what we really look like. Bile rises in my throat. I'm sure I'm about to throw up. This is what the others look like. Do I look like them?

The sick feeling subsides.

Now I feel a stirring within me; a feeling of warmth and emptiness. I'm both scared and exhilarated. For the first time ever, our bodies share the same space.

I swallow.

Then I do something... something I never believed I could ever, ever do. I reach out to touch Zumi's cheek.

It feels warm. Soft.

Just as quickly, I withdraw.

My finger tingles from where it made contact.

Zumi isn't an avatar. She's real. We're all real.

This is us.

The mascs watch with open mouths as my action makes them also realise that we're no longer avatars. We're in our actual bodies. We're real. Help! This is REAL!

Is this what we really look like?

A giant shiver runs down my spine. So many fears race through me. Will we catch each other's germs? Why are we here? Is this truly happening? Is it just a dream? A nightmare? How will we ever survive? What if we get the Great Plague? How come *ComCen* has left us here?

Too late. I stare at the others. The first thing that strikes me is how similar we are. Our skins are so clear, I can see each vein and artery, pulse and muscle. We have wispy white hair that falls onto identical wide foreheads; high cheekbones that taper to narrow chins, huge slanted eyes, and short noses with flared nostrils. Our mouths are well developed, the lips pink, soft and full. But our necks seem too long for our short and narrow bodies. Only our tummies are round. Though our arms and legs seem undersized in comparison with our heads and bellies, our hands are well developed. But they are far too large for our arms. Our fingers are long and slim. Our matching silvery coverall nanosuits make it even harder to tell us apart.

We stand in front of Rio's mirror. We can't stop staring. It's the first time I know what our bodies look like. Except for tiny differences it's hard to tell us apart. But when I peer more closely, I see that Jafet is slightly taller. Trist's jaw works up and down when he gets upset. Zumi's eyes are violet. Mine are so brown they seem almost black.

I edge slightly away from the others and slowly touch my head, shoulders, hips, thighs, legs. Then I bend over to feel my feet. The figure in the mirror copies me. Each movement is painfully slow.

The others wordlessly watch.

Then they do the same.

As one person, we turn. From the rear, we're identical.

What might have happened next is anyone's guess. Except that Rio swings out of bed and towers over us. She's tall, almost twice our height, and so much stronger, we openly cower. 'Are you aliens? Maybe you're hobbits or elves. Are you from Mars? You have to tell me what you are.'

Mars? We blink, bewildered by her questions. Jafet audibly gulps. 'No. We're like you. We are Homo-Sapiens and we live on the third planet circling the sun known as Terra.'

'Terra?' Rio's face clears. 'Earth, you mean.'

'Yes,' I say. 'We're from the future.'

'The future?'

'Yes.' Jafet frowns. 'What year is this?'

'You mean, what's today's date?' She frowns. 'It's the

fourteenth of March twenty, forty-three. If you're from the future, what year is it for you?'

Jafet smiles ruefully. 'By your calculations, it is also the fourteenth of March. But our year is twenty thousand and forty-three.'

She takes a long moment to absorb this. 'You mean... you mean... you're from the twenty thousandth century?'

'Yes,' Trist hurries to explain. 'That's why it's so confusing for you to meet us.'

'And for us to meet you,' I murmur.

Trist shakes his head. He starts one of his cartwheels… and hits the floor with a loud thump. 'Ouch!' Tears run down his cheeks. 'That really hurt.'

Jafet helps Trist back onto his feet. Both mascs are so clumsy they can barely stand upright without having to lean against a wall.

Trist's face contorts as he rubs his bruised back.

Jafet says, 'We're here to study you and your times.'

'Study us? Rio's eyes narrows. 'Like fossils?' She thinks this over. 'That's so rude.'

Rude? She's used that word again. Why?

No one knows what to say.

By now, made braver by our small size and obvious shock, Rio is over her original fright. 'I'm not sure I like that,' she says thoughtfully. 'Anyway, how did you get here?'

We tell her about our assignment. Rio listens carefully. She asks lots of questions. 'You're supposed to learn how to cooperate as a team,' she repeats. In the long silence I hear cars moving outside, the distant wail of a siren. Then to my astonishment she adds, 'In school we get exercises like that.'

Rather than question her too closely in case she considers this also as 'rude', we stay silent.

Her next question astounds us. She wants to know what we look like without our clothes.

Jafet looks at us three, shrugs and obliges by removing his nanosuit. We study him in silence. I wonder if he's going to ask Zumi to strip as she's sure to kick up a fuss, but he turns to me. 'Your turn, Pya.'

Everyone's eyes are on me as I remove my nanosuit. There's another long silence. 'Not too different,' Trist says at last. 'Only no penis.'

'Idiot,' says Zumi. 'That's because Pya's a fem. Fems are different. They have breasts and vaginas.'

'Pya hasn't got breasts,' Rio points out. 'Just a round tummy.'

I feel blood rush to my face. Is there something wrong with a round tummy?

'We don't know what breasts should look like,' Jafet tells Rio. 'Only what they look like in our avatars, and I suspect these are not accurate. Rio, I suggest that you show us yours.'

Rio goes bright red. 'You want me to strip?'

We all nod. 'After all,' Jafet points out. 'Pya and I have already done this for you.'

'Suppose so,' she slowly removes her pyjama top and leggings. We stared intently at two small roundish protuberances with pale pink nipples. Between her legs is a cluster of very short hair. Also when she lifts her arms I glimpse more fine hair. She's not quite like our avatars, she's too short, too slim, her legs too long, her buttocks too narrow, though I can see that she might resemble them when she's a few anniversaries older.

She quickly pulls her clothes back on. 'You look about six. How old are you really?'

Jafet frowns slightly. 'In your years we are exactly thirteen.' Then he thinks to ask, 'Do you know about being thirteen?'

50

Rio smiles. 'All of you?' We glance at each other and nod. Her smile widens. 'Then we're the same age, Charlie and I turned thirteen yesterday. I bet Pya and Zumi will soon grow breasts and body hair like me. And like Charlie, the guys' voices will break and you'll also get face and body hair.'

Voices? Face hair?

What is she talking about?

Rio runs into Charlie's room. There's a long silence. Though we listen for the inevitable fight, we hear an excited, 'You've got to be having me on...'

Rio quickly hushes him. Next Charlie, his eyes on stalks, is in Rio's room. Instinct makes me hold up my hands to protect my face. I expect Charlie to hit out for getting him into so much trouble. Instead, once he gets over his initial shock and amazement, he asks so many questions, we hardly know how to answer them. We tell him a little about *The Great Disaster* and *The Great Plague*, and why we must live in separate Cells, why we only communicate through avatars and holos. But there's so much that we ourselves don't know or understand.

How did we get here?

Why has *ComCen* stopped all contact?

Why have our avatars disappeared?

Why are we experiencing reality?

Why is reality so uncomfortable?

It's Jafet who thinks to make Rio and Charlie promise not to tell anyone about us.

Charlie looks disappointed. 'Why not?'

Because we know so much about Ancient Times, about how destructive humans are at present, and how much worse it will get, we glance at each other and shake our heads. 'Better no one knows what is going to happen,' Jafet says at last.

'Not as if it can be stopped,' I add.

'And if others find out about us, they might punish us for bearing bad news,' Trist says soberly.

We talk and talk before we finally convince Charlie this is for the best. I also use the opportunity to examine Rio's Cell. Where mine is tiny – just enough room for my sleep-chair pods and function-pods, this space feels enormous. And busy – the walls lined with posters of what I later learn are Rio's favourite music groups, family holos set inside frames that constantly change and another smaller Viewing Machine. Her shelves are packed with manikins, some furry like the one she gave Emma. The floor is covered in colourful rugs, also furry, and more games, these much bigger, that include a long handled object used for hitting red balls with white stitching, small balls... middle-sized balls... all size balls. And shoes. Rio has so many, all shapes, colours and design. We Hatchlings have never worn footwear. Our feet are short, square, with round toes and very pink toenails, the skin on our soles and heels as soft as our tummies.

Rio's room tells me lots about her, and what sort of fem she is. I decide that I would like to know her better. Hopefully, not all fems are as difficult as Zumi.

At last Charlie says, 'So you live in separate Cells. No mothers or fathers. Only a giant computer you call *ComCen* and tutor-holos to look after you, this is the first time you have ever been together, and you have only ever talked to each through your avatars...'

'Plus you get loads of schoolwork,' Rio buts in. 'You work all the time. Never get any time to fool around. You poor things.'

She seems to feel sorry for us. I wonder why.

Footsteps come past. Rio signals for us to crawl under the bed. 'What's all that noise?' the Mother calls. 'Why is Charlie in there?'

'Uh...' Rio gulps. 'Uh... He's helping me with an assignment.'

'If you don't get to sleep, tomorrow you'll be very tired.'

We wait for the Mother to walk away before crawling out from under the bed. Jafet says, 'Rio, tell us about your learning Cell.'

She does, occasionally interrupted by Charlie. It's hard to picture a Cell so enormous that has far too many out of control germs. 'We miss being with our friends,' Rio sadly ends up.

'Only till this siege is over,' Charlie says gruffly.

We don't know what to say. Slowly, gradually, we get used to being together. But we still can't touch. Reality is too difficult. I don't think I will ever get used to it. When I think back to when I suggested I wouldn't mind experiencing it, I smile wryly remembering how horrified Zumi was, and how right she's turned out to be.

Eventually Rio asks, 'If you only ever were able to see each via your avatars, how come you're here?'

We all talk at once. 'As far as I can tell, this has never happened before,' Jafet finally sums up. 'It's all quite unaccountable, extraordinary, and there's no logical explanation... none at all-'

'*ComCen* must've broken down,' Trist adds. His jaw quivers. Stuck in this fragile body, he seems even more upset than the rest of us at losing his avatar.

'And we don't know how to get back,' Zumi says between sobs.

Tears run down my cheeks. The other three are also weeping.

What will happen to us now?

Rio yawns loudly. 'Well, I'm too sleepy to stay up any

longer.'

'So am I.' Zumi's sobs turn to hiccups. So I do something that's never happened before. I place my hand on Zumi's knee. The contact feels warm. Secure. Comforting. It must be for her too, because she doesn't push me away.

Charlie yawns loudly. 'I'm half asleep.'

'Tell you what,' Rio offers. 'Zumi and Pya, you squeeze into the other end of my bed. Trist and Jafet, you can sleep in Charlie's room.'

She hands us a box of soft white paper. I used one piece to dry my eyes. Jafet and Trist do the same, though Trist pretends to blow his nose. Zumi stops hiccupping. We make an effort to pull ourselves together. Rio asks, 'Anyone need a bathroom?'

After she explains what bathrooms are, we creep into a room where the floors are so slippery it's hard to stay upright. I hold my hand under a tap. Nothing happens. I use all my strength to give it a wrench. Water gushes out. This water feels cool and slick. I let it run through my fingers, watch how it bubbles, rises and falls, then taste it. Twenty-first century water is sweet, yet not too sweet. It's quite unlike the water we drink on our Cells with its bitter underlay. I cup my hands, fill them, then drink and drink. Amazing! Straight away, I feel better.

Then I twist the tap the other way. Ouch! I quickly pull my hand away. Hot water hurts. I try the cold tap again. Running water over my hands feels similar to when I'm under a sonar-wash-tube, only more so. Everything feels so new, so weird, so disembodied, though it's really quite the opposite.

But I don't want to waste any more energy on being frightened. Instead I turn taps on and off. So much fresh water seems nothing short of a miracle. We have to ask Rio how to use the toilet. We take turns and she shows us how flush it. More water runs through. We watch it bubble up and descend. If I half expect to hear Jafet lecture her on the importance of conserving water, I think he's just too tired.

Straight after this, Zumi and I fall into Rio's bed and we're so exhausted we're asleep almost before our heads touch the sheet.

9

Evacuation

In the middle of the night I wake to a loud banging. Heavy footsteps stagger downstairs. We climb out of bed, crouch on the landing and peer between the balustrades.

Downstairs, the Father looks through a small hole in the front door.

'Open up,' a harsh voice yells. 'Police!'

Father takes his time. Three Terra-police enter. Visors cover their faces. Each is holding a laser and wearing a holster with several hand guns. One says to the Father. 'A state of emergency has been declared. We're evacuating everyone.'

First, there's a stunned silence. Then everyone springs into action. Mother runs into Emma's room. Rio and Charlie race back to theirs. Father calls, 'Bring warm clothes.'

Alarmed, we watch the Family get ready to leave.

What will happen to us now? Still nothing from Tutor-Henny or *ComCen*. If the Family leaves us here, we'll never cope. We'll die. The other Hatchlings look equally upset. Eventually Jafet pipes up, 'Rio, do you have any idea of where we can reside in safety?'

She looks dismayed. 'Can't you go home?'

We shake our heads. Our hearts thump. Our teeth chatter.

Rio bites her lip. 'Well, you can't stay here. Best come with us. But you look too different. I'll find you other clothes.'

In Charlie's room, she grabs pants and jackets and hands them to Jafet and Trist. Back in her room, Zumi and I drag pants, sweatshirts and parkas over our nanosuits. Rio's clothes are so big, though we roll up our sleeves and leggings, the bottoms keep falling.

'Shoes.' She tosses some our way. 'See if they fit.' My feet feel like small fish in large ponds. Rio hands us knitted caps. 'Pull them low so people can't see your faces or those buttons on your heads,' she orders, and when Zumi starts to protest, 'Don't argue.'

Even Zumi knows when to shut up. I'm too terrified to open my mouth. Outside, copter searchlights pick out anything that moves. About twenty police copters block the road. I watch those cars without copter adjustments, packs loaded on top, head in one direction. It stops my breath. Where have I seen all this before? Wasn't it the holos I'd viewed of the beginning of *The Great Disaster?* Can this be happening? Why has *ComCen* left us here at such a dreadful time?

As the Father unlocks the car, the Mother catches sight of us. 'These children… who are they?'

Charlie looks uncertain. 'Oh… ah… They're the quads. They live further down the street.'

'What are they doing here?'

'Poor things, they lost their parents.'

The Mother settles Emma on her hip. 'Well, we can't leave them. They'd best come with us.'

Charlie pushes us into the back of the car. 'Crawl under the seat,' he whispers, 'so no one can see you.'

The Father joins the queue leaving the district. Crouched on the floor, all I can see are telegraph poles. No lights. Only a fingernail moon mostly hidden behind cloud.

We drive to the other side of the city. Trying to avoid a traffic grid-lock, Father makes a quick left hand turn. Three blocks further, the car splutters to a stop.

'Battery's dead,' he mutters. 'Won't be anywhere to plug it in.'

'Can't stop here. Far too dangerous.' The Mother's cheeks are grey with fear. 'We'll walk.'

The Family climbs out and sets off. We four do our best to follow, though it quickly becomes too hard. Thankfully, the twins walk slowly with us.

'How come there's no energy?' Trist whispers to Charlie.

'Street gangs steal it all.' His voice rises. 'If I was older, I'd never let them get away with it.'

Father has waited for us and he hushes his son.

We step into a street lined with burnt out buildings. A tin clatters onto the road. My heart almost stops. Someone is watching us. An image of that scary Terran woman from the funfair pops into my mind.

'Weirwolf?' Trist tries a tentative skip. He's quickly learning to move less awkwardly. But I know he's scared because his voice wobbles.

'Arachnida?' Zumi is openly rigid.

'Betelgeux Shape-Shifter?' If so, we've no chance of survival...

A half-starved dog slinks out of the shadows. We heave loud sighs of relief.

Father strides off with Emma strapped to his back. Mother walks alongside him. Charlie and Rio stay close behind. 'Try and keep up,' Charlie urges. We do. But our movements are too slow. Our feet hurt. The soles of our feet are too soft. Soon our heels and toes are covered in blisters. We're barely used to walking. We've never worn shoes before. And now we have to run.

Mother and Father rush ahead, every so often yelling to their hatchlings to move faster. Though we follow as quickly as we can manage, the distance between us widens. The final straw is when Zumi trips over a gutter and falls. She lies there sobbing. Tears dribble down her cheeks. We stare at her in dismay.

Trist is furious. 'Zumi, get up! We'll lose the others.'

'Can't,' she whimpers. 'My ankle... hurts... shoes too big...'

No one knows what to do. 'You're such a pain!' Trist goes to hit her. Only footsteps heading towards us stops him.

I'm so scared liquid dribbles down my legs.

Charlie and Rio appear out of the shadows. 'Pya, Zumi, Jafet, Trist...Where are you?'

I nearly faint with relief. 'H-here.' My voice wobbles. 'We're here.'

'Come on,' Charlie yells. 'We have to get away.'

'Zumi has a sprained ankle,' Jafet calls. 'I observe that it is swelling to double its normal size. She is now unable to walk.'

'Oh no,' Charlie groans. 'We'll have to carry her.'

The mascs manage to carry and then drag Zumi a little further. No light. It's pitch dark. Not only have we lost Father and Mother, we keep losing each other. The twins keep testing their wrist-phones but can't connect. Charlie cries, 'If you're from the future, don't you have some way of calling each other?'

'No,' Jafet gasps. 'Our avatars interact without our help. We've never had to use an instrument like yours.'

We blunder on until Charlie walks straight into a car left in the middle of the road. A man lies beside it, blood pooling around him. He's very still. Charlie stoops to feel his throat. 'He's dead.'

Is this what death looks like? I glance nervously around. I'm sure his killer is somewhere out there watching us. What do we do now?

Charlie is wearing boots. He takes one off, wraps his coat around it and uses it to smash one of the windows. Then he reaches in and opens the door. We climb in. Jafet says, 'Is it permissible to take this vehicle?'

'Well, that man won't be using it,' Charlie says dryly.

Rio calls, 'Can you start this car?'

'Not without unlocking the computer,' he mutters.

We sit there wondering what to do. I'm so scared, my heart feels as if it's about to jump out of my chest. My belly turns to liquid. I'm sure my nanosuit stinks.

'This engine is very primitive,' Trist says unexpectedly. 'I can make it work.'

Rio and I push him into the front seat and we help him pull out the dashboard. Inside is an incredibly basic computer. He fiddles with it.

At first nothing happens. Trist shakes his head. He tries again. To our relief the engine turns over and gives a loud roar. Trist tries a few switches. Lights turn on. We inspect the fuel gauge. Charlie says, 'There should be enough energy to drive to a fuel outlet that will get us out of the city.'

'How?' Zumi shrieks. 'How, if we can't program this car to

drive itself?'

'So we drive it manually.'

'Sez you!' Trist is ready for another row. It doesn't help that Rio chimes in with, 'We can't drive this without the computer.'

Trist thinks this over. 'So we do this together, huh?'

He sits on Charlie's knee and steers, while Charlie operates the pedals. The car jerks away. As we bump along an uneven road, my forehead hits the front seat. I feel it gingerly. Now, on top of everything else, I have an extremely sore head. We head further into the suburbs. Every street is empty. Eventually we come to a three-lane highway where cars form bumper to bumper lines.

'Another grid-lock,' Charlie mutters. 'Wouldn't you know?'

Rio stares through the windscreen at cars lined up like ants. 'What now?'

Trist and Charlie manage to edge into one line of cars leaving the city. But at the first intersection, we're forced into another lane as it moves slowly along, every so often coming to a standstill.

Finally Rio wails, 'Where are we going?'

Charlie stares stonily ahead. 'I say we head for the sea.'

'No way,' Rio wails. 'Look! Everyone's turning the other way.'

'Exactly. Let's try and reach the coast. We can stay there till things calm down.'

Tears dribble down Rio's cheeks. 'But what about Mum, Dad and Emma? We'll never find them.'

'We'll come back later.' But no matter how much Charlie keeps promising that they'll return to find the rest of their Family, she can't stop crying.

10

Driving into the Country

Somehow Trist and Charlie manage to manoeuvre the vehicle along the road until the traffic starts to ease off and they can build up to a little speed.

Dawn – I wake to Trist leaning on one shoulder, Charlie the other. My heart gives an unpleasant jolt. Who is controlling this car? I climb over the back of the seat into the front. Jafet is on Rio's knee. He steers while Rio handles the foot controls. 'Easy when you figure out how.' She points to the controls. 'If the car's computer is disabled, this pedal makes the wheels turn. That one stops it.'

The road winds between grassy banks lined with bracken. Beyond those banks, I glimpse green expanses which, Rio assures me, were once used to graze cattle and sheep.

Right now those paddocks are empty.

'Most animals were killed for food.' Rio explains. 'When I was little there was always heaps to eat.'

'What happened to change things around?'

'There was a war and all the food got sent to the soldiers. Meant we had rationing... could only buy small amounts of everything. Shortly after, street gangs took over the City and grabbed any supplies left over. Then it just got too hard, lots of people got sick and died...' She sighs.

Knowing that this will only get very much worse, I reach forward and tentatively place a hand on her knee.

She gives me a quick smile.

'Where are we?' I ask.

She looks uncertain. 'I reckon we should be somewhere near the coast.'

By now everyone is wide awake. Jafet steers the car around the next corner and says, 'Viewing the sea will be extremely interesting. I look forward to seeing real waves dash against the shore. Then there's the tide's ebb and flow to consider, plus all that complex marine life to examine. But what will we do for shelter and food once we arrive?'

Charlie shrugs. 'Dunno.'

We consider this. I try not to panic. Now my belly as well as my head hurts. All I want is something to drink and eat. It's hard to believe that I once took shelter for granted. Hunger and thirst are most unpleasant. I'm missing Tutor-Henny... missing my comfortable life back in my Cell... asking why all this is happening to us...

'I'm hungry,' Zumi wails. 'I need a food-tube. When do we eat?'

'Stop it, Zumi,' Rio cries. 'We're all hungry.'

'Yeah.' Trist can never resist baiting Zumi. 'You're not the only one that's hungry and thirsty.'

I glance at Jafet. He doesn't say anything. Nor does he try to calm the others down.

Zumi sulks, but for once he doesn't yell back. A few curves later, paddocks stretch into swamps flanked by sand hills. Beyond the sand hills, I glimpse a vast greyish-blue expanse. It takes me a long moment to realise this is the sea.

It should make us more cheerful, except right then the car slows down and stops. Our battery is dead.

We climb out, our movements stiff and awkward from being so long in a small space. Even the simplest action seems to take forever. Poor Trist is even unhappier. He so hates being trapped inside his real body.

'Don't leave anything behind,' Rio warns. We collect our jackets, caps and Charlie's pocket-knife. Rio finds a torch and matches in the boot of the car. Then she heads for the beach. We trip over stones and clumps of weed as we blunder after them. Walking is just sooo hard. To think that I wanted to know what it might feel like to touch, walk, run and swim. Right now I can't believe how stupid that was.

We head towards a picnic area. Further on, we see the charred remains of a building. 'Must be the local Life Saving Club,' Charlie dourly explains.

We inspect the blackened ruins. Trist asks, 'How did that fire ignite?'

'Probably Snouts,' says Rio. 'They're into lighting fires.'

'My belly aches,' Zumi wails.

'Mine too,' says Charlie. 'We need to buy food.'

'Got any cards?' Rio asks sarcastically.

Charlie face falls. 'No. Have you?'

She turns her pockets inside out.

'In this century,' Jafet carefully explains. 'Cards must be exchanged for food.'

I sigh loudly. Did I once pray for something new to happen? If I'd known how frightening that could be, I would definitely have been happier with the way things were. My mind's eye pictures Tutor-Henny's calm eyes, soft pink cheeks and round body. Right now I'd give anything to have her hover between food-tube, chair, desk and sleep-pod singing 'Time wasted is time lost'.

We wander across the grounds. Grass seeds attach themselves to my outer clothes. Soon they poke right through Rio's pants and parka, and into my nanosuit. Those seeds scratch my tender skin. A strong wind brings tears to our eyes. We pull down our hats and zip up our jackets. It's still very cold. We trudge on and on. Finally we come to a strip of yellow sand. At the far end, a rocky shelf stretches into the sea. Behind are caves, the largest at least fifty times the size of Cell Q3. In it we find empty cans and the charred remains of a fire.

Rio straps Zumi's sprained ankle with a dirty rag she found in the car. 'Let's stay here,' she tells Charlie.

'No fresh water.'

'There's a tap back there.'

We return to the picnic grounds and turn it on. Brownish liquid trickles out. We're too thirsty to be fussy, so we do our best to ignore its noxious colour. I tell myself not to notice its foul taste, not to worry that it might make us feel even worse. We're so hungry we'll eat almost anything. At low tide, Charlie, Rio and Jafet walk out onto the shelf to search for shellfish. Using Charlie's pocket-knife, they prise tiny sea creatures called mussels and black pipis out of sea-weedy pools. Meanwhile Trist helps me gather grass, twigs and driftwood to make a fire. Every action is exhausting. Even though the wind freezes my ears and numbs my fingers, I'm covered in perspiration.

It takes us ages to light that fire. In the process we use up most of the matches. But once we have a decent blaze, we throw the shells onto the fire and wait for them to pop open.

All this time Zumi never stops complaining. 'Don't see why we had to stop here. I'm cold... I'm tired... There's nowhere to lie down... my leg's sore... Why can't we look for some place further on-'

My eyes roll.

'It's okay for you, Pya,' she says spitefully. 'You haven't got a sprained ankle... you don't know how much this hurts... I bet you'd be a pain if something happened to you...' Her nose wrinkles at the smell. 'Ugh. They make me want to throw up.'

I just shrug. Though these mussels taste truly weird, I'm so hungry I'll eat almost anything.

Rio turns to me and asks, 'Is she always like this?'

I shoot her a despairing look, and then stare out to where choppy waves roll onto the shore.

Zumi reddens and falls silent.

I continue staring out to sea. A few minutes later, Rio and I join the mascs. We leave Zumi behind. She picks over a few mussels, but doesn't eat any. I think about asking her to join us. Then change my mind. I tell myself that if Zumi's unhappy, she's only got herself to blame. Anyway, I like being close to Rio. It makes me feel special.

We spend only one night in that cave. It's cold and damp and the floor is so hard. Sometime before dawn, something wakes me. Trist, eyes closed, is yelling, 'Keep away... stay away from me...'

I lean over and shake him. 'Shhh, Trist. You're dreaming.'

His eyes spring open. 'Wha...what's going on?'

'You're having a nightmare.'

'Oh... ugh... thanks.' He sinks onto the floor.

We both go back to sleep. Then I'm back in Cell 34Q listening to voices I've heard before:

'Are they ready?' First Voice asks.

'Not nearly ready,' says Second Voice. 'They still have a long way to go.'

'But their bodies are cold and hungry. What if they get sick?'

'They may suffer a little. But if something unexpected happens, we know what to do.'

'And there is no other way to ensure that the same tragic events won't be repeated? Would not travelling through the wormhole be enough?'

'Absolutely not. Only through great personal effort and understanding can another Great Disaster be averted.'

'So... How will we know when to bring them back?

'When....'

I start up. Those voices... I could swear they belong to Tutor-Henny and *ComCen*. I lie there puzzling over my dream. What can it mean? What if this is part of *ComCen's* plan? Didn't *She* hint that this exercise was to force us to work together as a team? Might all this be under her control? But what if it isn't? What if *She's* blundered? What if *She* can't bring us back? I remember those holos we saw of The Great Disaster. Back then billions and billions of people died. And we've been catapulted right into those times. How will we ever survive? Aren't the odds just too great?

I give myself a mental shaking. These thoughts will get me nowhere. Still brooding, I drift back to sleep.

Some -time later my eyes open to light seeping into the cave. The others are out on the rock-shelf. I'm so stiff I can barely stand up. The others return with handfuls of pipis. 'Reckon we should look for houses,' says Charlie.

'We didn't pass any on the way here,' Rio reminds him.

'Who asked for your opinion?' her brother retorts as if this is somehow Rio's fault.

'Pig!' She shoots him a ferocious glare.

I just stare. How can we survive in this hostile place if even the twins keep fighting?

'I suggest we travel in the opposite direction,' Jafet chimes in.

'What about Zumi's ankle.' Rio turns to her. 'Reckon you can walk?'

Zumi gulps. 'You going to leave me here..?'

'Yeah, yeah…' Trist's cheek quivers. 'If we do, it serves you right for being such a pain.'

Zumi bursts into tears.

'Do stop provoking her,' Jafet mutters. 'Cannot you see how distraught she becomes? I hardly think that this treatment of our weakest Hatchling serves any positive purpose.'

'Still…' Charlie looks Zumi up and down. His frown made him seem very grown-up. 'We can't keep carrying her.'

'Well.' Rio's hands settle on her hips. 'We certainly can't leave her behind.'

Everyone talks about Zumi as if she isn't here. She sobs loudly. 'Maybe I can try and walk.'

I know I should feel sorry for her. But I don't! Doesn't she always moan and complain? Isn't she the most self-centred argumentative fem ever?

Before Jafet can smooth things over, Trist says sourly, 'Yeah, yeah, just keep annoying us.'

Tears roll down Zumi's cheeks. Maybe it isn't all her fault that she doesn't get along with Trist. He can be quite nasty when things aren't going his way. But I keep this to myself. I don't want him turning against me, so I help Zumi onto her feet and wait for her to thank me. Instead, she wipes her face on her sleeve and limps away. I can't believe how ungrateful she is. Serves her right if the others treat her badly.

We collect our things, store what's left of the pipis in Charlie's cap, and set off, Zumi leaning on Jafet's shoulder. Charcoal clouds threaten to drop their wares. We pass the burnt out Life Saving Club and turn onto the road. From there, we backtrack the way we came. When we arrive at the t-junction, Charlie leads us in the opposite direction.

PART 3

BUSH-WISE

11

Learning to Walk

As we trek through the countryside in a constant search for food and water, soon the mascs are too tired to support Zumi.

Jafet finds her a good strong stick and she manages to limp behind us. The road weaves through scrub and t-tree. I find walking difficult. Soon I can barely manage to place one foot after another. My thighs and calves won't stop trembling. Every muscle aches. It doesn't help that there are too many steep hills. To add to this, Trist and Zumi continually squabble. They never stop. Not for a moment. We've hardly gone any distance before Zumi plops onto the ground. 'Can't walk,' she moans. 'My ankle hurts too much.'

'Listen to her,' Trist jeers. 'Never stops complaining.'

'You haven't got a sprained ankle like me,' she throws back. 'Anyway Trist, you're not so special. Who woke everyone last night with a nightmare? You're such an avatar breaker,' she shrieks.

I flinch. This is the worst thing she can call him. They glare at each other. Fortunately, Rio and Charlie are too far ahead to hear, and Jafet's stopped trying to keep any peace between us four. He just plods on. I'm so fed up, I yell, 'You two keep fighting and we might as well give up right now.'

Trist stalks off. Zumi slowly gets back on her feet. I struggle along two paces in front, my feet slipping and slopping in those oversized shoes. My toes and heels are covered in blisters. When I remove my right shoe, one blister oozes blood. Rio inspects my feet and shakes her head. She pulls off one of her socks and tells me to wear it. I'm so grateful, tears roll down my cheeks.

'You need to practise walking,' she tells me.

'Practice. You mean, like practising plasto-steel synth?'

'What's that?'

'Music,' I explain as I stagger along. 'The music I write.'

'You mean like playing a keyboard? Or a guitar?'

I shake my head. 'I just think up sounds and *ComCen* produces them for me.'

'You mean, you don't really have to play any instrument?'

'No. *ComCen* does that. *She's* given me perfect pitch.'

'Lucky you!' Her tone is envious

'Yes well, except...' I hesitate. 'We never get any time to ourselves. Tutor-Henny follows *ComCen* orders, and She expects us to only work.'

'What if you didn't? What if you rebelled?'

My chin drops. This has never occurred to me. 'But... but *ComCen* never, ever allows us to disagree.'

Rio blinks. 'Never?'

I shake my head. Then nod.

'You poor things.' She sounds rather sorry for us. Given that this is beginning of *The Great Disaster*, I can't help wondering why. Before I can explore this any further it turns out she wants to know more about my synth. 'Maybe one day, you can play me some?'

'Maybe,' I say. But without *ComCen* to produce the sounds, I can't see how.

We walk a lot farther. Not that we ever meet any cars or people. Not even any animals, only a few seagulls. I'm sure I can't manage one more step when we come to a sign reading *Bayside Animal Reserve.* A gravel road leads into it. Charlie visibly brightens. 'I know this place.'

'Which species inhabit this territory?' Jafet asks.

'Koalas, wombats, birds, insects.'

I remember some holos I've seen of Ancient Times. 'Will there be kangaroos and possums?'

Charlie smiles tiredly. 'Guess so.'

'How about snakes?'

He laughs. But I shiver. I remember that lethal snake in Ancient Times, the one that only needs to touch you. Every holo claims certain snakes kill.

'Look!' Rio points ahead. 'House. Behind those trees. Maybe someone's home?'

Trist pushes ahead. 'Hang on,' Charlie yells. 'We don't know who's in there.'

'So?' Trist stops, puzzled. 'Won't they provide us with food and drink?'

Charlie catches up. 'What if they aren't friendly? Best take it quietly. Follow me.'

We crouch behind some bushes. From here the house looks deserted. Grass and weeds are waist high. Eventually Charlie decides it's safe to look through the windows. Once we're sure the house is empty we see one window has been left ajar. Between us we manage to prise it open. Charlie gets us to hold him up while he looks inside. 'Bathroom,' he calls. 'Help me climb up.'

Once in, he unlocks the front door. Rio runs into the kitchen and turns on a tap. Clean water gushes out. She checks the pantry. 'Lots of food. We'll be fine.'

I help her open cans of baked beans and tuna and packets of biscuits. A shelf contains bottles of liquor. We don't bother with those. I discover that beans slide down easiest. Not that there's anything wrong with our teeth. But we Hatchlings are still learning how to chew. Later when I mention this to Rio she says, 'Only food-tubes. Lucky you've got any teeth.'

I peer into the mirror to examine them. 'They seem fine.'

'Mmm,' she admits. 'Whiter than white. And so straight. Lucky you, not having to wear bands. Still…'

But this is only when we know each other better.

Right now, and only after we can't swallow another mouthful, do we explore the rest of the house. 'Probably used for overnight stays,' Charlie finally declares.

This hut is certainly basic even by Ancient Times standards. There's a large room with a double bed and four bunks, and off that, a small bathroom. No electricity. Only a large wood stove and several lights that Charlie tells us only work by pouring a liquid called kerosene into glass and metal lamps. Two of the living-room walls are lined with paper-books. Most contain information on local plants and animals. 'Ranger's cottage,' Charlie decides. 'Wonder where he's gone?'

Rio says sharply, 'What if he's a she?'

Oh no. Not another brawl. Only Jafet jumping in with 'Let's hope she won't mind us making ourselves at home,' stops it happening.

Our first task is to light the stove to heat water. The previous occupiers have left us cut-up pieces of wood. I find towels, material we use to dry ourselves, in a cupboard. That evening, Rio fills the bath and Zumi and I climb in. Sitting in water is interesting. I observe how it slides off my skin. Note its resistance and movement. This much water seems a complete miracle. Rio shows us how to make soap bubbles by squeezing arms and splashing. She helps us wash our dusty hair. 'Fancy this being your first bath ever. Pya, how do you manage to stay clean?'

'We use sonar waves.'

'Sonar? Cool.' She points to my head. 'That button. What does it do?'

'It's there to help us remember things.'

Rio bites her lip. 'Hide it under your cap. Best warn the others about this, too. You don't want anyone asking awkward questions.'

'Sure.' I'll agree to anything that keeps us safe.

'Tell me what your avatars looked like?'

So I describe Zumi's avatar, her black waist-length curls, smooth dark skin, black as a berry eyes, perfect nose, high cheekbones and rose-bud lips. I tell her how mine had a lithe full breasted body, slender hips, extra-long legs, cornflower blue eyes and waist length golden locks. But a little while later after we climb out of the bath, and I glance at the mirror, I see a fem with white, short wispy hair, translucent skin, dark brown slanted eyes, and a nose, mouth, lips and chin too large for a heart-shaped face, a neck too long for a short, weak body. How I wish I looked like my avatar.

Rio gets me to describe again how we lived in tiny Cells where our tutors did everything for us, how we worked all the time, how we only ever went anywhere via our avatars.

She says, whilst towelling herself dry, 'How come your suit fits like a second skin?'

'It'll fit anyone who wears it.'

She holds it up, marvelling at how the suit can shrink to the size of my hand and then expand. 'Can I try it on?'

'Sure.'

She stands in front of the mirror watching the suit grow and wrap itself around her. 'All those shimmering colours. All I have to do is think them in. How does it work?'

I redden slightly. How come I've never bothered to find out? 'You can think it into any colour or style you want,' I say quickly. 'It keeps the wearer warm and snug.'

'Great,' she says. 'Cool, isn't it Zumi?'

Zumi coughs. 'Only an old nanosuit. '

She hasn't said a word all night and now she's feeling left out. Well, that's her own fault. If she wasn't so difficult and demanding, this wouldn't happen. She slides back into the water and closes her eyes. Rio and I glance at each other. There she goes again, we silently agree. 'Rio,' I say, 'Something I keep meaning to ask?'

She grins. 'Fire away.'

'What's it like having a Mother and Father?'

She doesn't answer right off. 'Sometimes... like when they're fighting or hassling you, I wish I was anywhere else. Other times…' tears glisten on her eyelashes, 'you miss not having them around.'

Poor Rio. I'd like to comfort her, only I don't know how. I turn to ask Zumi for help, but she's busy blowing bubbles.

I turn back to Rio. 'What's it like being a twin?'

She zips up her jeans before saying, 'Most of the time it's okay. I never feel like I'm alone. I mean, I know we fight a lot. But if anything should happen to Charlie, I think I'd die. It's like he's my other half.'

'Does that mean you always give in?'

'No way. That's why we fight.'

I stare at her, puzzled. 'So what's so terrific about that?'

She thinks how to answer this. 'Guess because we were born at the same time to the same parents and we've never really been apart. Also I'm good at math and science, and Charlie's great with languages and humanities. I love playing sport, but Charlie prefers experimenting with technology. So I help him out when he's in trouble and he helps me, that way we manage okay. And if any outsider has a go at either of us… we'll always protect each other. '

'Do you have other Hatchlings?'

I have to ask this again before she understands.

'You mean friends? Of course,' she says indignantly, 'heaps. But Charlie and me, we always protect each other. We're a team.'

Like us? Rather, like what we should be. I glance at Zumi who has finally climbed out of the bath. But she's busy examining her swollen ankle.

The next two days it hardly stops raining. When it does, I practice walking. Trist often comes with me. So does Jafet. We line our sloppy shoes with paper to make it easier. Determined to keep up with the twins, we do our best to strengthen our thighs, ankles and feet. Soon, our walking is so much better.

While we walk, we talk over what's happened and try to make sense of it. Trist's theory is simple. 'I reckon *ComCen's* broken down.'

I'm shocked at the suggestion. 'But… but *ComCen* never breaks down.'

He shrugs this off. 'In the end *ComCen* is only a machine. A machine can break down any time.'

'So you think we're here forever.' My heart sinks because I always hope *ComCen* will take us home.

'Back to the same boring Cells and doing everything via our avatars,' he reminds me. 'You really want that?'

I suddenly realise that I don't, and shake my head.

A little later I approach Jafet with the same question. He doesn't dismiss my fears as quickly as Trist. 'In my opinion,' he says, 'this might be part of *ComCen*'s plan…'

'Which is?'

'To force us to work together as a team.'

'Well, we're not, are we?'

He sighs. 'No, we're not.'

'Can't you make Trist and Zumi get on better?'

He smiles wryly. 'Can you?'

At least we see lots of animals. Once there's a terrible noise like nothing I've ever heard before. I'm terribly scared. What if this is a monster that's planning to catch and eat us? My avatars have fought too many endgames with terrifying creatures like Weirwolf, Arachnida and the Shape-Shifter. Then I glimpse a fat animal blinking sleepily down at me.

I tell Rio.

'Probably a male koala,' she says. 'They can sound very angry. Here,' she searches through the shelves until she finds a book about local animals. 'If you see anything new, look it up.'

I take this book wherever I go. I recognise an echidna. And once a small mob of wallabies hop close enough for me to catch their gamy smell. I learn to watch out for scratchy twigs and biting insects. Once I find a luminescent greenish blue beetle. When I take it back to show Rio, she says, 'A Jewel Beetle. Pretty isn't it? Best return it to where you found it.'

I do. The house is remote enough not to worry about unexpected visitors. With plenty to eat, drink and somewhere to sleep, we feel relatively safe, though I miss the comfort of Cell Q3. If I look back at how Tutor-Henny anticipated my every mood, how easy it had been to never take responsibility for any action, it seems that I had lived another life that was never totally mine.

On the fourth day over a meal of canned tuna and boiled rice, Rio cries indignantly, 'I'm sick of doing everything. Tomorrow, Jafet, it's your turn to fix meals. Charlie, you clean up and Trist and Pya, you two have to stop the stove going out.'

Zumi looks hurt. 'How come you never include me?'

'Isn't your ankle still too sore?'

'Typical Zumi,' Trist jeers, his jaw working up and down. 'Always gets out of everything.'

Zumi turns on him. 'Who says?'

Mostly because I feel bad about not spending more time with her, I spring to Zumi's defence. 'Having a sprained ankle makes things hard.'

'Okay, okay,' Jafet chimes in. 'Zumi, I suggest you help Pya and Trist to keep the fire going.'

Zumi's lower lip trembles. 'No one does anything to help me get around.'

This time she's gone too far. 'That's so unfair,' I yell. 'Don't I help you out of bed and into the bathroom?'

'I always have to ask.'

'There she goes.' Trist is openly sarcastic. 'Nothing's ever good enough.'

'Hey,' Rio chimes in. 'Stop fighting, will you?'

'Right,' says Charlie. He stands over Trist in a mock threatening way. 'If you don't stop teasing Zumi I'll throw you in the water tank.'

We all giggle.

'For all I care,' Zumi says viciously, 'you can all jump in and drown.'

Hurt, I turn away. After all I've done for her?

'What's up, Zumi?' Rio asks, puzzled.

She bursts into tears. 'You two keep going off, leaving me behind. And,' she venomously adds, 'Pya thinks she's so good, but she's always judging others.' She yells, 'Take a good look at yourself, huh?'

I glare back. How come Zumi's so horrid? Trist is right. She only ever thinks about herself. The rest of that day, everyone goes off by him or herself. Then, because fighting is exhausting, next morning everyone sleeps in. By the time Trist and I check the stove, we're out of wood. We wheel a barrow out to the woodpile and start filling it with logs. Something thin and black wriggles out.

Snake!

Trist's eyes follow my finger. He freezes. We stand there, trembling and helpless.

Cornered, the snake shows us its spiky tongue.

Liquid trickles down my legs.

Suddenly something cracks down hard. Zumi is hitting the snake with her stick. The snake doesn't appreciate this, because it slides back under the woodpile. Both Trist and I are still too frightened to move. Seconds later, the snake slithers out and takes off into the bush.

I'm rigid with embarrassment. Now the danger is over, I feel sick with relief. 'Thanks, Zumi,' I finally manage.

'Um...er... thanks Zumi.' Trist's face is as grey as Zumi's stick.

In the bathroom I wash away my embarrassment. I'm so upset and ashamed. 'Don't be silly, Pya,' Zumi says. 'Anyone would be scared.'

I try hard to believe her.

Trist is waiting for us to come out. He shifts from foot to foot. 'Um... ah... that was real brave. Zumi, reckon we can be friends?'

She doesn't answer right off. 'Promise you won't tease me anymore?'

'Promise.'

She holds out her hand. 'Friends forever.' But just as their palms meet, I hear engines roar up the drive.

12

Snouts

Three motorcyclists drive up to the door and dismount. My chin drops.

Three boars with human bodies.

The boars pull off their helmets and turn into fems.

Though we'd never seen these fems before, from all that Charlie and Rio have told us, we know what they are.

'Snouts,' Trist mutters.

Rio, Jafet and Charlie race in from the kitchen. Everyone trembles. Rio and Charlie have already told us about this street gang. Snouts think nothing of trashing and setting fire to property. They're known to maim and kill people. The twins claim that meeting any Snout has to be the worst disaster ever.

'What now?' Rio wails in a tiny voice.

Charlie makes for the back door. 'Quick. Before they see us.'

'But there's nowhere to hide...'

'Just do it.'

We race into the garden shed. Crouched under the tiny window, we watch three fems walk into the house. But we've left shoes and jackets in the kitchen, clothes in the bedroom and unmade beds. They'll know we're here. The Snouts spend a few minutes inside before one comes out the back and heads towards us.

I stare at her in disbelief.

It's the fem-holo I saw in *Cave of the Unknowns*. Only in real life she's even more terrifying. She's so huge, she has to turn sideways and duck to fit through the door. She has waist length dreadlocks, ridged eyebrows, little eyes, wide cheekbones and pointy metal teeth. A tattoo covering her right shoulder shows a boar with extra-long tusks.

Someone calls from the house, 'Anythin' out there, Fobia?'

'Heaps,' Fobia answers. 'Come an' see for yourself.'

The other two make for the shed. Fobia kicks open the door. She towers over us. I close my eyes and wish, oh so wish myself back in my Cell hearing Tutor-Henny sing 'Time wasted is time lost'.

'Well, well...' Fobia's metal teeth glint evilly. 'Nego, Oomf, take a lookit these weirdoes.'

My chin drops. If Fobia thinks we're weird, what is she?

Nego pushes her aside. 'Heh, heh, whad ya know. Kids! Whad we gonna do wit''em?'

We stare wordlessly back. Though Nego is half Fobia's height, she's as broad as she's tall. Metal pigs pierce her nose and scalp. More dangle from her ears. Oomf is equally frightening, but unlike the others, maybe because she's smaller, she's somehow less threatening.

'Kids!' Nego's spit hits the floor. 'Wasta time.'

'Yeah,' says Oomph. 'Send 'em packin'.'

Nego shows us her fists. One reads H.A.T.E. So does the other.

'What d' ya know...' Fobia squeals. 'I always wanted to eat human flesh.' She pinches my arm so hard, her fingers leave bruises, and her bony knee digs into my neck so I can hardly breathe. 'This one'll taste like chicken or piglet.'

Next, she's bolting the door from outside.

We're still inside.

We're prisoners.

Zumi and I crouch on the floor. My heart gallops. I'm so frightened I think I'm about to throw up. The other Hatchlings are equally scared. They squat on the floor and close their eyes, as if by not seeing, they can make this nightmare go away. Only the twins keep constant watch. Rio reports back to us when the Snouts go into the house. Soon, they find the ranger's bottles of liquor. We hear loud laughter and the sound of glass being smashed.

'What now?' someone whispers.

Rio turns to Charlie. 'Can you get through this window?'

'No way. Maybe Pya can. She's the littlest.'

I gulp loudly. My hands and knees won't stop shaking. 'I can try.'

Charlie and Jafet lift me up onto the bench. The window opening is tiny. Charlie spits on his finger and cleans a patch of glass so I can peer outside. He says, 'We'll try after dark.'

'Those Snouts...' Jafet clears his throat. 'Where might they come from?'

Charlie shrugs. 'During the war lots of parents were killed. Kids who survived joined tough gangs. The fiercest joined forces and turned into Snouts.'

Minutes become hours. Meanwhile we turn the shed upside down looking for something, anything, to help us get away. All we find are boxes of newspapers and magazines and some coats and shoes that smell musty. We try to find clothes that will keep us warm. My mind churns over these past events. Why is this happening? Surely this must be some strange decision on *ComCen*'s part to leave us here. But what if Trist is right and *ComCen* has broken down? What if we're stranded here forever? If only I could talk to Tutor-Henny. But my tutor is just one arm of *ComCen*. If *She* has broken down, this means Tutor-Henny is equally powerless.

Meanwhile Rio does her best to keep us calm. She uses balls of string to teach us a game she calls catspaw. 'Tie the ends together and hold it across your fingers. Now slip your middle finger in and turn the string around.'

We spend the next few hours practicing catspaw and keeping watch on the house. For once, maybe because we're so scared, anytime a quarrel starts, the others quickly remind everyone to stay quiet.

By mid-afternoon we're terribly thirsty. 'Might have to drink our own pee like when people are shipwrecked,' Charlie is saying when Oomf suddenly appears carrying a bucket of water and three large cans. She closes the door quickly behind her. 'Water n' food. Don' mind a little horsin' around,' she adds shaking her bullish head and dusty dreadlocks. 'But first things first. Kids aren't s'posed to starve to death or be eaten.'

No one dares speak.

'So open your ears n' lissen,' she fiercely continues. 'I'm gonna leave this door unlocked. It's up to you what you wi' it. Only…If Fobia catches you, I dunno nothin'. Okay?'

We glance at each other and nod. She closes the door behind her, makes a big pretence of turning the key and heads back to the house.

We drink all the water and empty the cans. Then we empty our bladders and bowels into the bucket. In this hot little shed, soon the smell is sickening. The next few hours seem to go on forever. So does the party inside the house. As the shadows grow longer, we hear a sudden blast. Three... four times...

A cry as if someone is hurt.

Then? Nothing.

The silence is deadly.

One by one, the kerosene lamps in the house are lit. Hours later, they flicker out. Only when there's nothing more to see or hear, does Charlie dare open our door. It creaks loudly. Convinced that the noise will alert Fobia, we wait and listen. Our hearts thud so loudly, we're sure she can hear them. No moon or stars. It takes ages for our eyes to adjust.

'Follow me,' Charlie whispers and heads into the bush. We do. Snakes, spiders and other creepy crawlies seem safe compared to what waits for us in the cottage. We have to get away.

13

Lost!

Clouds scud overhead. We come to the road. Rather than risk our footsteps being heard on crunchy gravel, we stumble through the bush to fall over roots and blunder into prickly bushes. Charlie leads. But his torch is back on the kitchen table so this escape is not only scary but risky. Each time someone steps on a crackly twig, my heart gives a huge jolt.

Jafet heads into a stump. Trist crashes into him. 'Watch out,' he yells. Everyone tries to hush him. But Trist is so scared, he lopes ahead making it harder for the rest of us to keep up.

We walk into more blackberry and trip over unexpected clumps of bracken. Even though my nanosuit usually protects me, prickles manage to wriggle through. Soon my ankles are scratched and bloody, my feet covered in blisters.

Finally we come to a small clearing. Charlie says, 'Let's

wait here for daylight.' I watch him through half-closed eyes. In the space of a few days he's grown up a lot. It's hard to recognise him as the same young masc who bickered with his twin and was angry with his Mother and Father. Rio is also more grown-up. Not only does she comfort Zumi who keeps breaking into hysterical tears, she almost manages to keep Trist calm.

I can't imagine anything worse than this night. I try to sleep on the hard earth between Rio and Zumi, but an owl's hoot sends my heart into my mouth. Animals rustle in the bushes. Ants and beetles scuttle around us.

'Only possums,' Rio decides when we start up at a dreadful growling.

But I keep remembering that thin black snake. What if it's just waiting to attack?

I mention this to Jafet. He reminds me snakes sleep at night.

It doesn't make me feel better.

Half way through the night, it starts to drizzle. We open our mouths and drink. The drizzle turns into a downpour.

'Why is it always raining?' Zumi wails. 'I'm always wet... cough... cough... Back in my Cell it never rained...'

Finally, even Charlie can't stand her any longer. 'Least you're wearing a nanosuit that keeps you warm and dry,' he just about explodes. 'My clothes are soaked right through. I'm ever so cold.'

Rio tries to quieten things down. 'Me too. But we'll dry out later.'

After that, no one else dares complain.

Irritable and scared, we sleep lightly. We're up at first light pushing through scrub towards the highway and Rio is right as our clothes quickly dry. A little further we come to a crossroad. She asks, 'Which way?'

Charlie spins a stick. When it stops spinning we take off in that direction, only stopping every so often to let Zumi rest. At least Trist, Jafet and I can keep up with the twins. This way we drift further inland, our only water, puddles from the previous night's rain. Soon our stomachs start grumbling.

'Look for bush tomatoes,' Charlie suggests.

'Not even the remotest possibility,' Jafet says gloomily. 'From my research I know bush tomatoes only grow in the desert.'

We do find a few blackberries, but they're dry and sour. Then we find a tree bearing little green apples. That's a mistake, because soon we have sore tummies and are squatting behind bushes.

The further we walk, the more it seems we're heading right into the bush. No signs of civilisation. No waterholes or creeks. By now we're seriously thirsty. With daylight starting to fade, Jafet calls a halt. 'I'm exhausted!' He sinks onto the ground. 'My limbs are incapable of managing another step.'

Rio settles in beside him. 'Let's stay here.'

We make a wind-break out of branches and bark and curl up under it. The others fall asleep almost immediately. Though I'm bone weary, I can't sleep because even in my nanosuit, pants and parka, I'm terribly cold.

Too many thoughts trouble me. There are so many things I don't understand. Why has *ComCen* deserted us? Is Jafet right? Might it have something to do with this exercise? And if so, surely we're not meant to die from hunger, thirst or Snouts. But what if, between *ComCen* dropping us here and now, *She* can't bring us back? Angry and resentful, I do finally fall asleep because magpies carolling at dawn wake me.

14

The Children

Though the sky lightens to a lovely soft pink, I'm too stiff and sore to admire it. Every muscle aches. It takes ages to get back onto my feet. There's no sign of Rio or Jafet.

'Where to now?' Zumi moans. I wait for someone else to tell her to shut up. No one does. No one has the energy to squabble.

'Guess we just keep walking,' Charlie mutters as Jafet and Rio appear from behind a clump of trees.

'Find any water?' I call.

Rio shakes her head. 'No.'

'No creeks, not even a puddle,' Jafet adds, too worried and upset to expound in his usual way.

'Can't be helped,' Trist says sourly.

Charlie nods. 'Can't worry about finding water when we

have to get as far away from those Snouts as possible.'

Though the prospect of the next few days sounds bleak, I keep reminding myself there must be some positives in all this havoc. I might be exhausted, thirsty, hungry, my face starting to peel from too much sun, but certain things have improved. Even though my feet are covered in blisters, my legs are strong enough to keep up. Sometimes I even lead. Soon we come to a gravel road. A little further, we reach a crossroad. Trist squats and asks, 'Which way?'

'Dunno.' Charlie leans against a tree. 'Rio, what do you reckon?'

She shakes her head. 'Jafet, you choose.'

Jafet looks carefully around. No houses or farms, only vast tracts of bush that rise across steep virgin hills. He finally points in a different direction and says, 'Water always travels downhill. We would be more likely to come across a creek if we travel that way.'

No one disagrees. We plod on and on. We're too tired and thirsty to talk. My throat feels raspy. My mouth is choked with dust. Though the country we're moving through is very beautiful, I have no energy to admire it. No creeks or waterholes. Not even where the road levels out. My easy life back in Cell Q3 feels like a dream. But was it? Light-headed from thirst, I'm confused as to what is Actual, Virtual, or merely imagination. What if all we're going through is only a nightmare? What if this is all *ComCen*'s way of testing us? What if we have no understanding at all of what is happening to us, only the discomfort we feel?

Soon Zumi sinks to the ground. 'Can't walk. My ankle hurts too much.'

Trist's face is a study. 'Leave her here,' he manages through clenched teeth.

'That's not possible,' Jafet points out. 'The odds of Zumi surviving on her own are completely negative. Such a resolution should not even be considered.'

'Get up,' Charlie yells. 'Get up or I'll hit you…'

Only Rio and Jafet rushing in stop him.

'We can't stay here with her,' Charlie yells. 'If we don't leave her behind, we'll all die.'

'Yeah…' Trist completely forgets his previous promise to be nicer to Zumi. 'She only ever thinks about herself.'

'Don't be stupid,' Rio cries. 'Course we can't go on without her.'

'Zumi,' I insist. 'You've got to keep going. Get up, will you?'

How can she give up so easily? How can the others even think about leaving her behind? I yank her back onto her feet. Now with her leaning on my shoulder and then on Jafet's, we walk and walk until the sun is high overhead.

A sound, an unfamiliar sound comes towards us.

The rattle of wheels on gravel.

Oh no. Not more Snouts.

Heart in our mouths, we hide in the bush and stay quiet as possible. A dusty gravel road is just in front. We hardly dare breathe. Gradually the sounds grow louder. We hear voices. 'How about that?' Jafet whispers.

Two caravans. A dozen or so adults pull them uphill using ropes and chains. Small children run alongside. Their progress is so slow we have time to study them as they move past us. Three mascs. All are grey bearded and shaggy haired. They wear pants and shirts made of possum fur roughly stitched together. I count five fems. One is old and white haired. There are four young ones. Two of the young fems have hatchlings strapped to their backs. Apart from decorating their hair with feathers, the fems also wear possum fur pants and shirts. All three mascs and any fem not carrying a hatchling, also carries a weapon.

We watch them push and shove those caravans up the next incline. It's a sweaty, slow process. We wait for them to be safely past before Charlie says, 'They might have water.'

'What makes you think they'll share?' Rio whispers back. But Charlie has already decided we have no choice but to meet them face to face. He steps out of his hiding place and stands in front of the first caravan. We follow at a safe distance, ready at a moment's notice to run.

Their leader sights Charlie, aims his weapon and cries, 'Stop or I'll shoot.'

Charlie holds up his hands to show he's unarmed.

My breath catches in my throat. What if the masc means this? What will happen to Charlie?

'Over here,' the masc orders.

Charlie does as he's told. 'I'm lost,' he calls. 'Do you have any water?'

The masc doesn't lower his weapon. 'Any more of you?'

Charlie nods. He signals for us to show ourselves. We trickle out from behind the trees and line up beside him.

This is one time being small serves us, because as soon as the man gets a good look, he lowers his weapon and exclaims, 'Kids! What are you doing here? You alone?'

'Yes… Snouts,' Rio half sobs. 'We had to run away. They said… they were going to eat us…'

The masc, whom we soon learn is Thomas their leader, gestures at us with his other hand. We must still look odd because he frowns slightly. 'What are they?'

'Them? They're the quads. Me and Rio, we're twins.'

My heart hiccups. Thomas continues staring. He's obviously unconvinced. 'How old are they?'

'Thirteen... Ah... four.'

'Hmm. Unusual colouring. Test tube babes no doubt. Devil spawn.'

No one dares argue. What if he tells us to go away? What will we do then?

It's our good luck that the older fem with white hair, whom we later know as Judith, steps forward and says briskly, 'Poor little things. What does it matter if they're devil spawn or not? They're children aren't they?' She turns to us. 'Come, you need something to drink and eat. We haven't sunk so low as not to care for lost kids.'

But the man isn't easily convinced. 'How do you know this isn't a trap?' He points to the bush. 'There might be others.'

Judith turns to Rio? 'Are there? You'd best tell the truth. Thomas always means what he says.'

Rio shakes her head and bursts into dry sobs.

'Course not.' Judith's voice is kind. 'I can always tell when kids lie.' She climbs into a caravan and returns with a water-bag, a loaf of bread and a hunk of sun-dried meat. As Rio and Charlie hold out their hands she says, 'Before you drink and eat you must thank the Lord for all He provides.'

All the mascs and fem drop to their knees and place their foreheads on the ground. There's a long silence. Judith looks up and frowns. Seems we're expected to do the same. Once we do, Thomas raises his arms heavenwards and prays, 'Thank you Lord for this bountiful meal. Without your care and loving devotions these youngsters would have nothing.'

Only then does Judith hand the water and food to Rio. Never have we needed these so badly. Only when everything disappears does Thomas look us over again. 'Why are those children so fair?'

'Their parents come from Sweden,' Charlie says quickly.

'Swedes are very fair.'

Thomas looks faintly disbelieving, but he doesn't argue. He introduces his followers. 'That's Joshua and Samson. The women are Judith, Rebecca, Naomi, Ruth and Mary, all good Bible names.'

Though I don't know what he's talking about, Charlie and Rio nod furiously. Not wanting to appear different, we do the same.

'We call ourselves The Children,' Thomas explains. 'Because the world has fallen into such evil ways, we Children live a simple existence and travel the countryside in our gipsy caravans. Are you prepared to join our group in His service?'

We all nod. We have no choice but to agree with everything he says. His gaze sends a shiver down my spine. Thomas isn't someone I'd ever dare cross.

'It means you must pray with us, help us find food and water and move these vans. If you agree, we will share our resources with you.'

Though I want to ask if carrying the latest laser-gun is returning to a simple existence, of course I don't. Rather we keep up the pretence of being very young, far younger than Charlie and Rio, and leave any negotiating to the twins

15

What went wrong?

It doesn't take long to get into The Children's routine. Five times a day we kneel, place our foreheads on the ground and listen to Thomas pray for forgiveness and thankfulness that we've survived. Though he continues to view us Hatchlings as 'Devil Spawn', his companions like Rio and Charlie enough to share what little food and drink they have with them. The twins in turn share what they're given with us. They even find us a tent so we no longer have to sleep in the open.

We don't understand what these 'sins' are that Thomas talks about. When we ask Charlie to explain, he says, 'I always thought sins were bad stuff we did ourselves.' But it appears that according to The Children, their idea of 'sin' covers everything to do with these terrible times we're living in, and little to do with individual acts.

Most of the time Thomas seems to ignore us. Only once do we get the feeling that he might send us away. We had gone past what had once been a pretty village that was now empty. It was hard to know what exactly had happened here as little was left except a few blackened walls. Only one was semi- intact. On it was a half-torn poster advertising an old time movie. It fluttered in the breeze. The twins stared at it in amazement. As they later explained, it seemed utterly strange to find a reminder of their previous lives in this sad place. Charlie was carefully removing it so the paper wouldn't tear any further when Thomas caught him at it. 'You take that piece of idolatry,' he said fiercely, 'and you will all stay here.'

Charlie gulped and walked quickly away.

We learn a lot more about The Children. Our second night as we sit around the campfire, and all praying and eating is over, Thomas says, 'Once I worked in advertising…'

Later Rio explains that his role was to persuade folk to exchange money for products they possibly didn't need.

'… where I led a sinful life where I used more natural resources than I could ever reproduce,' he continues. 'Our world went from bad to worse. Then one day I realised that it was sinners like me who have reduced the world to this sad state. All I could do was return to a life that was totally natural. I spoke to Joshua and Samson and between us we agreed it was time to return to basics. In other words, to live as one might have lived before machines were invented.'

I listen very carefully. That evening in our own tent, I whisper to the others, 'Why does Thomas feel responsible for everything that's gone wrong?'

'Not everything,' Rio whispers back. 'Maybe he just feels that we didn't share what we had with poorer people in other countries. That's what triggered off The Great War and its nuclear aftermath. This country was lucky in that no nuclear warheads were sent here, but we were bombed. Many people died. Then bad people took over the cities...' she throws up her hands in a helpless gesture.

Trist asks, 'How does he explain gangs like the Snouts?'

But Jafet doesn't try to find an answer for this. He's still pondering Thomas' reasons for setting up his Children.

'Possibly Thomas is somewhat responsible,' he opines. 'If he did encourage folk to needlessly use up Terra's resources, then surely he must, to a certain extent, be held accountable.'

Trist doesn't agree. 'Don't see how one person can do all that.'

'Didn't you see how angry he was when we found that poster?' Rio reminds us. 'He went on and on about how movie stars should share the responsibility of making kids think becoming famous and spending heaps was important.'

'He sure got mad.' Trist giggles. 'Set the poster on fire and stomped around it. He's got a serious temper.'

'Guess he feels too many folk have been cheated,' Charlie points out.

'If enough people feel cheated,' Rio says slowly, 'they get angry and finally this boils over. Then you get what Dad calls 'anarchy and lawlessness''.

'Thomas doesn't trust us,' Zumi chips in. 'He never makes eye contact.'

Charlie bites his lower lip. 'That's because the other day Jafet, you remember how windy it was? You forgot to wear a hat and he noticed your head button,'

Jafet reddens and turns away. I don't dare open my mouth in case I'm later sorry for what I say. Isn't Jafet always telling us to be careful? Why doesn't he listen to his own warnings? I take a few calming breaths and ask, 'Why does Thomas calls us Devil Spawn?'

Charlie looks thoughtful. 'Maybe he thinks you've been created in a lab.'

'We were,' I murmur.

'Well, he obviously doesn't think this is natural.'

'He hates us,' Zumi says faintly. 'Only Judith stops him sending us away.'

I stare into the dark. Not being with Charlie and Rio is too terrifying to think about. Rio must pick up my thoughts, because she says firmly, 'Whatever happens, we mustn't let anyone separate us.'

'Right,' adds Charlie. 'Our only hope of survival is to stay together.'

'And maybe finding Mum, Dad and Emma.'

Charlie doesn't say anything. But in the failing light of the fire, I watch him put his arms around Rio to comfort her.

***

One day follows another and all are similar. All our energy is used in hard work. There are caravans to pull, food and drink to be found. Sometimes we're lucky enough to come to a farm where there are still people. We pick fruit and vegetables and the farmer pays us with produce. Once we're given a basket of duck-eggs in exchange for clearing a paddock. Seems there's no longer any use for money or cards.

After a while Zumi stops complaining about her sprained ankle, so I guess it no longer hurts. Anyway, no one is interested. We're all too worn out by trying to stay alive. Between prayers, meals and sleep, we push those caravans over hills and valleys in a constant search for water, food and safety.

Thomas is a good shot and sometimes we're lucky enough to find game and help him skin and cut up a kangaroo, a wallaby or a possum. Then we roast or dry the meat over a fire. Every so often we come to hidden valleys with fruit bearing trees. When there's no other food, we fems gather wild grasses and pound them to make a coarse flat bread. Life is hard and we often go hungry, though we usually find water.

More often we come to deserted farms and hamlets. Once, we arrive at a sad village where each house hides bodies in an advanced state of decay. We dig a mass grave and bury these nameless people. Though no one dares say this aloud, we all worry that we might also get sick. Thomas spends a long time praying, pointing out that it was their life of sin that led those sad villagers to this state.

'More like a virus that's gone through several mutations,' Jafet mutters under his breath.

We beg him to stay quiet. What will happen if Thomas overhears? He's sure to send us away. Then how will we survive?

Because Jafet is interested in ancient cultures, he watches the group very carefully. 'Each adult fem is committed to a monogamous relationship with one of the mascs,' he told us, 'but the mascs have polygamous relationships with several fems.'

'Oh no,' Rio groans. 'Can you say that in plain speak?'

Jafet reddens, and apparently consults his language knowledge. 'I mean, these three men have more than one wife.'

He's right. I never quite manage to sort out which hatchling belongs to which fem and masc. All adults and older children act as 'Mothers' and 'Fathers' when it comes to the younger ones, and all are treated with equal warmth. They are also equally chastised if they disobey.

But not everything is bad. Between being worked hard, we still have time to observe different varieties of trees and shrubs, how certain grasses find cracks and crevices, how in damp places pale green moss is soft as possum skin. We quickly learn to beware of stumbling into a bull-ant or a jumping-ant nest, to swat away pesky bushflies that drink our sweat, and squash mosquitoes that feed on our faces and hands. Flocks of different coloured birds fly overhead as if what's happening on the ground doesn't concern them.

Sometimes we come across a swarm of bees and the bravest mascs raid their hives for honey. On hot nights, the cicadas warn of another scorching day. If we're lucky enough to find a pond or creek that's still running, tiny fish dart between stones. Jafet often joins me as I lie beside the shallows. As we watch multi-coloured dragonflies skim over the water, he almost forgets to keep talking.

It is the butterflies that most entrance me, because they remind me of that lovely village I went to in my meditations back in Cell Q3. At night in our tent when my body aches with tiredness and I remember to meditate, I recall a riverbank bordered with weeping willows that leads to a park lined by shady maple trees. This path takes me to a pool where huge goldfish swim from side to side, their plump bodies courting the afternoon sun. The various scents of jonquils, narcissi and jasmine mingle. Birdsong and bee-buzz fill the air. Birds and butterflies colour it. From here I look onto a village's main street straddled by a mossy stone bridge, see thatched roofs just beyond. These memories finally lull me to sleep.

****

Thus many weeks, even months, pass with us travelling with The Children. Occasionally we meet other refugees. They usually came from the cities where they report total lawlessness. All are suspicious of strangers. Dangerous folk roam the countryside. Thomas makes sure anyone we meet knows we're armed. If we have any food and drink to spare, he'll give them some. But there's something so fierce about him, most strangers take off very quickly.

Only once is there a confrontation. This time the stranger is even scarier than Thomas. His face is badly scarred, his shoulders slung about with rifles and lasers. What makes things more frightening is that the stranger wields a machete.

Thomas warns him off with several shots. But this stranger is determined to ransack our caravans. There's an ugly scene when both fire at each other. The stranger's shot is wide off the mark. Thomas aims his laser at the other's feet. Fortunately he misses or that masc would have limped forever. It scares him off, but it also acts as a warning never to try anything that might upset Thomas.

As if we don't already know.

16

Sickness and Death

None of this stops us bickering between ourselves. Jafet still talks over everyone and never listens. Zumi's bad moods don't get any easier. Though her ankle is quite whole, she uses it as an excuse to get out of work. Trist takes every chance he can find to be nasty. I get so fed up with both, I pretend they aren't with me.

One day Zumi accuses me of flirting with the twins. My jaw drops. 'Flirting?' I say indignantly. 'Don't know what you mean.'

'You act as if everything Rio and Charlie say and do is perfect. You think you're so good. Take a good look at yourself, huh?'

'Don't know what you're talking about,' I yell and stalk off.

What is she talking about? Not my fault she isn't getting

on with the others. It's not my problem. Let's face it, she's quarrelsome and self-centred.

She's just too hard.

But if I'm being totally honest, the others aren't much easier. Trist will start a fight over anything. He particularly likes goading fems, always telling us we're not pulling our weight work-wise, which, when it comes to me and Rio, is simply not true. Jafet loves the sound of his own voice. Sometimes I think he talks even in his sleep. We're always telling him to shut up. Then he looks totally hurt.

Rio spends a lot of time helping the older fems look after their hatchlings. She's also gone back to looking so sad she makes me want to cry. Because Charlie is also expected to do a grown man's work, he's always tired. All he does when he's not working is eat and sleep.

I try to stay outside everyone's moods, and keep some kind of balance. Not that it does me any good. One day Zumi yells, 'You're so judgemental, Pya. All you do is watch and criticise. But you never look at yourself. You suck up to whoever you think will be nice to you. You're such a hypocrite!'

I don't talk to her for days.

As for Thomas and his Children – all I see is a group of people who follow his every order, no matter how unfair. He never stops referring to us as 'Devil Spawn', and I sometimes I see him eyeing Rio in a way that sends an uncomfortable shiver down my spine. I know Rio feels this too, because one day she says in this flat voice, 'I think Thomas wants me as another wife.'

Charlie's shudder matches hers. 'Over my dead body,' he mutters. But if we stay with the Children, what choice will she have?

The constant work and walking takes their toll on our

bodies. Our muscles ache, our arms and legs are scratched and often bleed, the skin on our faces peels from too much sun. Sometimes I'm grateful that there are no mirrors to examine my appearance. Only watching the other Hatchlings tells me how bedraggled we look.

One breathtakingly hot midday Charlie and I are sheltering in the shadows when he unexpectedly says, 'I keep wondering why you four were born.'

'You mean hatched?'

He nods.

'Well, why were you?'

He smiles wryly. 'Guess we just came because of Mum and Dad having sex. But *ComCen* must have hatched you for some reason.'

I stare into the distance. 'Maybe that's the way all babies will come in the future.'

'If so, what's happened to the grown-ups?'

I shake my head. 'How would I know? I don't even know what will happen to me when I'm too big to live in my cell.'

'Maybe that's why you were sent back here.'

'But… but that'd mean we have to stay here forever.'

'Maybe you do.'

Does this mean living through the rest of *The Great Disaster*? I can't bear even to consider this. Maybe there were other Hatchlings before us,' I muse. 'And if there were… what's happened to them?'

'Maybe they just grew up.'

I sit up to face him. 'So where are they now?'

He picks up a twig and plays with it. 'Who knows? Maybe they're all dead.'

We mull this over. Eventually he says, 'But you do know what'll happen to us in the future.'

'No. I don't. Least… not to you.'

'But you do have some general idea of the future of humanity,' he persists.

'I do know that what we're living in now is the start of *The Great Disaster*.'

He insists that I go into more detail. Though I hate filling him in, he isn't as shocked as I half expect. After everything he's already seen, this must be obvious. He says, 'Does this mean everyone will die? Like it'll be the end of mankind?'

'No,' I say. 'Some of you must survive because our ancestors built *ComCen*. There's thousands of years between now and the future.'

'Suppose so.' He frowns uncertainly. 'What if it isn't Rio and me?'

'How do you mean?'

'What if only other kids survive long enough to grow up and have babies?'

As this might be true, I can't think of any answer that might soothe him. Other questions trouble me. How come *ComCen* sent us to this family? Surely there has to be some reason to choose Charlie and Rio… some reason apart from us all being thirteen and born at the same time on the same day thousands of years apart. When I mention this to Charlie, he does seem happier. 'Maybe we do survive,' he says hopefully.

But there are still so many things we don't understand.

Next day I go to Judith to find another explanation. Of course I can't mention that we came from the future, so I just ask about her thoughts on life and death. She frowns and says, 'The Good Lord has his own reasons for keep us alive at such a terrible time.'

'But does that mean we have no say in it?'

'Course we do, but only to an extent.' Though her

weathered skin and coarse features don't resemble Henny's soft plump features, there's the same kindness, the same gentle manner, the same care. She says, 'Of course we must do our very best to survive if only to honour our Lord in prayer and pass on our beliefs.'

I respect her thoughts, but find little comfort in them. Following Thomas' strict code as blindly as his Children just makes me cross.

When I think back to how much I depended on Tutor-Henny, how often I threw tantrums, I get angry with myself. Back in Cell Q3 all I wanted was to make my own decisions instead of having *ComCen* do that for me. So it isn't until much later that something strikes me. When it comes to making decisions, isn't this happening to us right now? Aren't we being forced to learn and do for ourselves?

Several weeks pass like this. Most nights after the evening meal, I creep away by myself to study the night sky. Do those stars and planets echo my past life? I sit there thinking about *ComCen* and Tutor-Henny, wondering what's happening to them. What will next happen to us? Can we six survive *The Great Disaster?*

PART 4.

GLADIATORS

17

Running Away

For the next three weeks we spend a lot of time with The Children's five young mascs and seven little fems. Because we Hatchlings seem so much younger, we're not worked as hard as the twins. Any free time they have, Charlie and Rio research more tips about surviving in the bush. Then they pass what they learn to us.

Jafet and Trist try to make Charlie's work-load easier. They spend much of the daylight hours chopping wood to keep our fires burning, pulling carts, and searching for water and food. Though Rio works as hard as Charlie, she's often more miserable. I do my best to try and cheer her up. Nothing helps. Only finding her Mother, Father and Hatchling Emma will make a difference. But how can this happen? Every report we hear describes increasing chaos. We continue meeting other wanderers like ourselves. These mostly travel in small groups or alone. Once I get close enough to hide behind a bushy clump and listen to an elderly loner tell Thomas how bad things have become.

'So things are much worse,' Thomas rumbles into his beard.

The other man nods. 'Staying in the City is suicide. The only way to survive is to keep well away from other people. Anyway, the City has no more fuel or food.'

'So where is everyone going?'

The man shakes his head. 'All I can tell you is that millions of folk are searching for ways to stay alive. People are eating dogs, cats, rats.' He lowers his voice. 'I heard tell of a dead child-.' The rest is lost in a whisper.

Thomas' beard sinks into his chest. After a while he looks up to ask, 'What about any families?'

'Them too. So many families were lost in the last uprising.'

When I report this to the others, they become even gloomier. But Rio is worst hit. Observing her sadness makes me wonder what it's like to have attachments that can make a person this unhappy. Would I feel this way if one of us was lost? Not that Zumi's any help. If I suggest to her that she join us in helping the twins with their chores, she shakes her head and wanders away. She's the only Hatchling who does nothing more than what is essential.

'Just Zumi being her usual selfish self,' Trist acidly comments when I complain about her lack of cooperation. But is this so? Perhaps Zumi has decided that there's no point helping those as she views as unkind. I don't answer. Any mention of Zumi just sends Trist into a total rage.

That night I dream I am back in the City and running away from a soldier. If he catches me I am lost. I have already run so far, my lungs hurt, my breath is ragged, my legs weak and wobbly. The soldier uses my failing strength to catch and grab me. Now I look into his mouth, see his yellow broken teeth, smell his bitter breath and acrid sweat. Though I struggle as much as I can, I know what will happen. I know this man will tear me apart like a chicken or a rat and I will never survive...

Just as he starts ripping off my clothes, I wake with a start. I'm covered in a cold sweat. My heart pounds as if about to spring out of my chest. Just another nightmare, I tell myself. Around me the others sleep the sleep of the totally exhausted. Even though we spent all day searching for food and water until we could barely manage another step, it takes me ages to fall asleep.

Next morning when I mention my dream to Rio, she sighs and says, 'Maybe your dream showed what can happen if we get trapped in the City.'

We both shudder.

But not all is this bad. Some of the Children's older hatchlings teach us simple games as 'catch and tag' and 'hide and seek'. I like the baby Hatchlings best. One small fem is fair skinned with the palest hair. She reminds me of myself when I was little. I spend any spare time I can find trying to show how her to walk. When Rio comes across this, she laughs and says, 'Sandy has first to learn how to crawl.'

I find this interesting as I have no memory of crawling. I approach Trist with this question. He shrugs it off saying, 'Maybe we didn't. Maybe *ComCen* had us walking right off.'

Jafet says, 'It is more likely that *ComCen* had us creating our avatars and this is how we learnt to move.'

But no one can do more than offer other unanswered questions. Anyway, shortly something happens to stop us brooding about our own growing up. Some of the smaller children cough up blood and their breath sounds as if they can't take in enough air. One windy night Sandy is unable to move. Though the women stay up all night massaging her little chest, in the first light of the morning the little hatchling's breathing stops.

As they bury her next day, I can't stop crying. Is this what death is about? It's all very well to watch people die in holos. I always felt as if they had little to do with me. It was almost the same with the bodies we buried in the mass grave. But to know this hatchling and then lose her makes me so unhappy, I can't stop crying. Behind this misery is also the fear that this might happen to us. What if the others die and I'm the only one left? What will I do then?

I'm so unhappy I hardly notice that the others have more than a hatchling's death to worry about. Jafet frets that the sick children might have caught *The Great Plague* from those bodies we buried. Next day he calls us together. 'We have to get away before any of us also gets sick.'

Charlie is reluctant to leave. 'How do you know we haven't already caught it? We've been pretty safe here. We could be making things more difficult.'

'We four were dipped in a vaccine vat,' Jafet points out. 'But you, Charlie and Rio, haven't. This means you are extremely vulnerable to all kinds of infection. And if it's *The Great Plague*, none of us is immune.'

Rio looks slightly shocked. 'You think we should go right now?'

Jafet purses his lips. 'Indeed I do. Besides, Rio, you are in even greater danger from Thomas, aren't you?'

Her face whitens. She nods wordlessly.

'Well, I'm not leaving without food, water and a laser,' Charlie says grimly.

'Fair enough,' says Trist. This time there's total agreement.
'So we'll do it late tonight, okay?'

We glance at each other and nod.

We wait until after midnight to raid The Children's food supplies, but then we don't take much. This doesn't make us feel good. Haven't The Children shared what little they had with us? But Charlie manages to sneak into Thomas' tent and steal one of his laser guns. Then we disappear into the bush where we spend an uncomfortable night hearing danger in every sound.

Towards dawn night I hear those voices again.

'Surely they have suffered enough. Surely it's time to bring them back...' First Voice says.

'No.' Voice Two is firm. 'Not yet. They still have more to experience. Besides, they are still not co-operating. They're not pulling together as a team.'

The following morning I find Jafet and tell him all about it. All he does is grunt.

The next day and the next we stay well away from any road or track where The Children might be pulling their vans. We stray further and further into the bush in our constant search for water. We do find a trickle, but by then we've had nothing to eat for nearly two days. Even though we keep pleading with Charlie that we need to rest, that we haven't the strength to continue, he keeps repeating, 'We've got to walk as far as we can. Thomas will never forgive us for stealing his laser. He's sure to come after us.'

Only late into the second night as we keep blundering into prickly bushes and tripping over tree roots, do we stop running. Probably because we're so thirsty and exhausted, we collapse almost where we're standing and sleep until the night sky pales into dawn.

18

Weirwolf

My eyes open to a new and terrifying landscape. The first thing I notice is the cold. I can't stop shivering. I stagger onto my feet to see the ground is white. It takes me a long moment to understand that this cold white slippery stuff I'm standing on is snow. At my shocked cry, the others slowly wake. When they see what has happened, they spring to their feet. During the night we've been moved to a different place. We're standing beside a lake covered in ice. I've never seen this lake before. On the other side of the water, pine trees topped with ice crystals crowd towards snowy mountains rising into a pale grey sky.

By now the others are fully awake. When they realize how numb their faces, ears, fingers and toes have become, they wrap their arms around themselves and try jumping and down. Nothing works. They can't stop shivering. Zumi starts to cry, but as there's no wind, her tears turn to ice

Soon our hair and eyebrows are brittle with frost.

'This is just too weird,' Trist mutters. The rest of us are speechless. We can only stare at this strange valley. Charlie and Rio, who have never been shifted to different holos before, are rigid with shock. If once again I'm amazed at finding myself in a new place that's possibly on a different planet, my fear is nothing to what they must feel.

Once Jafet has had time to consider where we are, he says, 'My surmise is that, just as we found ourselves in the Twenty-First century, this is another instance of *ComCen*'s failure to return us to our Cells. Even if *ComCen* isn't working properly, *She'd* never expose us to any danger.' He turns to the twins. 'What do you think?'

But they're too upset, confused and frozen to come up with any answers.

Trist and Zumi are also puzzled, if not quite as much. All the different holos our avatars visited while our bodies were in our Cells help us cope with any unexpected change. But it's so much harder to convince the twins that they're just part of a giant computer breaking down. Almost paralysed by fear, they can only sit very still, very quiet, their stunned gaze taking in this wintry landscape.

'Got to get out of here,' Jafet mutters. Before we can question how and where, we hear a terrible whining-yowling. Wolves! Don't wolves live in snowy wastes? We look wildly around. Every turn seems to lead into more snowy drifts. But we can't stay here. If we don't start moving, our blood and lungs will freeze and we'll die. It's Jafet who yells, 'Come on,' and he sets off along the icy shore.

We follow, too cold and frightened to talk. Where can this

frozen lake lead? Rio recovers enough to mutter, 'Sunset, it's sure to get colder.' We watch a crescent moon rise behind the mountains. An icy wind that cuts through to the bone whistles around us. 'If we don't find shelter soon,' Charlie warns, 'we can't survive.'

We trudge on and on, sometimes tripping over clumps of frozen bulrushes and reed. Thirsty, we suck on handfuls of snow that numb our faces and hands. This lake seems endless. We keep walking, walking… We trudge on and on never seeming to arrive at anything new.

Just as we think this lake must go on forever, we take an unexpected turn and come to a rocky outcrop. Step by slow step, clinging to each other, we clamber over it, stumbling where the rock is jagged and sharp, until we come across a small crevice that opens into a cave.

Trist signals for us to wriggle into the crevice and inside. The cave turns out to be quite large. Right down the back we find a heap of firewood and four straw pallets. Best of all, beside the pallets is a very large hamper. Despite Charlie insisting, 'This could be a trap, there might be something dangerous inside,' Rio opens it. The hamper is packed to the brim with bottles of fruit juice, packets of biscuits, and cartons of food.

'This has to be *ComCen*'s doing,' I cry. 'I knew *She* wouldn't leave us to die.'

'Now necessarily,' Jafet points out. 'This could belong to someone else lost in the snow.'

The others are too tired and hungry to query this.

'First, we need a fire,' Trist mutters through frozen lips and heads for the wood. We start piling pieces together. As usual Zumi leaves this to everyone else. Instead of being grateful at what we've found, she moans, 'How are we going to light it?'

'Oh, do shut up,' Trist scowls.

Rio has already emptied the hamper and right at the bottom she finds a giant box of matches. While the mascs start a fire, Rio and I set out the food and drink. Careful printed labels tell us what everything is. When Rio presses a red button on one side, each carton heats itself.

I'm convinced this is *ComCen*'s way of making sure we survive. This is *ComCen* telling us that even if *She* can't bring us home *She* can, at least, keep us alive. But grateful to find shelter, warmth and food, the other Hatchlings aren't interested in who might have left this here. Only the twins remain openly wary. Charlie says, 'What if whoever owns this comes back and we've used all their stuff? They'll be furious. One of us must always stand guard.'

Though we Hatchlings believe this is *ComCen*'s doing, we don't contradict him.

'We have to watch out for whoever is making that terrible howling noise,' Rio soberly adds.

'Okay,' says Trist. 'I'll take first shift. Jafet you go next, then Rio, Charlie, Pya and Zumi. Okay?'

But then Trist wants third watch, so I agree to swap with him.

Of course Zumi has to moan, 'Why am I always last?'

'Thought you'd be grateful to get some sleep,' Charlie snaps back.

'There she goes again,' Trist jeers. 'Nothing ever is right for her.'

Zumi glares at both mascs, grabs one of the pallets, goes off into a corner by herself and spreads herself right over it leaving no room for me. As there are only three pallets left, Rio and I are forced to share. As they're only as wide and long as Rio, I'm terribly uncomfortable. One pallet might be big enough for two Hatchlings. But one pallet certainly isn't big enough for both me and Rio. Though I'm furious with Zumi, I can't be bothered to argue. What use would it do me? She'd only argue back.

After that, no one speaks to Zumi. When Charlie mentions that we're being unkind, I agree with Jafet's wry, 'She's just too difficult.'

We stay in that cave three more days. With enough wood to keep us warm, apart from my having to share Rio's pallet at night, we're reasonably comfortable. This much food means we can build up the strength we lost living with The Children. Though we take turns guarding our cave and often hear that mystifying howling-yowling, nothing happens.

Though Charlie and Rio never get over their shock at finding themselves here, Jafet keeps insisting to them that *ComCen* has probably broken down and therefore all *She* can do is help us six survive.

I'm not so sure. 'So why send us back in time in the first place,' I argue.

'Didn't *ComCen* inform us that this was an exercise in Archaeology?'

'Maybe.'

'And independent living,' he adds. 'Aren't we supposed to be cooperating as a team?'

I glance around at the cave's rough walls, the shadows our bonfire makes flickering against them, then at Zumi's hunched back. 'Well, that's certainly not happening,' I say with a wry laugh.

'It isn't funny,' he says grimly. 'More that it is frightening in the extreme.' Then, maybe because even Jafet is finding it hard to keep up his constant flow of talk, he briefly adds, 'Scary.'

'Yes, real scary.' I give a sudden shiver. Too many questions flood my mind. Why is all this happening? Should we expect another terrible event? And if so, can we come together long enough to overcome it? So much has happened since we were sent into the past, it's hard recalling our tiny Cells where our Tutor-Holos did everything for us, how we worked all the time, how we only ever went anywhere via our avatars. It seems another life entirely.

***

On the fourth day Rio and Charlie beckon Jafet outside. They talk a long time. When they return, Charlie gathers us together. 'We reckon we should move on,' he says. Look for a village. We should try and contact other people.'

'Too dangerous,' Zumi mutters. 'Maybe you haven't noticed, but there are wild animals out there.'

'Sooner or later we'll have no choice.' Rio points to an almost empty hamper. 'By tomorrow we'll be out of food.'

So packing the few food cartons and bottles we have left, we set off at first light around that frozen lake. We walk and walk, and hear an ominous crackling as the ice starts to melt and grow thinner. No clouds, only a pale wintry sun that lacks any warmth. By the time the sun is overhead, we're so tired we have to stop. Just as we've eaten the last of our provisions, there's that terrible howling- yowling, only very much louder. The sound echoes around the lake.

We can't stop trembling. That howl can only come from a wolf. But a wolf who calls this loudly must have a giant voice. And if he has a giant voice, this means he's also a giant. The only giant wolf I know comes from an endgame called 'Weirwolf'. Can this endgame be happening for real?

Trist signals for us to stay quiet. He points to the closest snow covered bush, and we hide behind. There's more howling-yowling. It comes from our right. The sound ricochets and comes closer. Suddenly a giant shadow appears from around a snowy drift.

Its owner follows it.

We stare, gape mouthed with fear. I was right! Before us is the Arctic wolf we know as Weirwolf. If this wolf is at least five times the size of any Terran animal, he has the same greenish-grey intelligent eyes, the same thick white coat, the same slavering jaws and, I remember from our endless game back in my cell, my stomach lurching, the same desperate hunger that means he will consume anyone he comes across. This time though, the Weirwolf isn't part of an endgame. This time he's real and waiting to attack. Though we do have Thomas' laser gun, I suspect it will be powerless against such a terrifying animal.

Like all wolves, the Weirwolf's ability to smell out his quarry is excellent. He stops and points his snout at where we're hidden behind a snowdrift.

Realising we're trapped Charlie steps out from behind the bush and aims his laser straight at the Weirwolf. Hoping to frighten him off, he yells, 'Stay away or else...'

The Weirwolf replies by more supplying us with more howling and yowling. Then he shows Charlie his slavering jaws and wicked teeth.

Charlie's response is to fire. The beam goes through Weirwolf. It makes no difference whatsoever.

Charlie keeps firing until he runs out of fuel. The monster pads close enough to stand in front of Charlie. There, he opens his mouth to howl and yowl again. The landscape echoes his triumph. If Weirwolves could laugh, I swear he's laughing at our stupid attempts to defeat him. Then he hunkers down and waits for the rest of us to come out from behind the bush. It's obvious he's planning to pick us off one by one.

All this time I'm trying to remember how we overcame him in our endgame. Back then my avatar dodged around him until he got so sick of trying to catch me, I was able to use my sword to give him that blow. But right now we have no swords. Back then our avatars were supple and agile. They could manage all kinds of acrobatics. But our real bodies, though a lot stronger, are still too slow and weak. In our favour however, back then there was only Zumi and me. Now we are six. Between us, there must be some way we can out-manoeuvre him.

I whisper this to the others. Trist catches on immediately. Even if Rio and Jafet don't agree, they're too frightened to argue.

Zumi whispers, 'What if one of us isn't fast enough? What'll we do then?'

'No choice,' I whisper back. 'The trick is to confuse him. Come on... it might still work.'

Meanwhile Charlie has been left to face the Weirwolf who merely stares back. We can't leave Charlie to handle this alone. Trist, who is still the most agile, murmurs a few instructions. The idea is to spring behind the Weirwolf, jump in front, and tease from every side. We must tantalise and annoy the Weirwolf enough to force him to leave.

We wait for Trist to yell, 'Go... get him... hit him...' And scooping up balls of snow we do just that. At first the Weirwolf seems astonished to see this many youngsters. He leaps around snapping at everyone like a dog trying to catch flies. We keep trying to confuse him. Trist springs in front, Jafet behind, and us fems dash around flicking snow into his eyes.

Though the Weirwolf is amazingly big and strong, his reflexes are slow. So he's tossing his head in annoyance and we have just about proved that he can't catch us, when Jafet makes the mistake of teasing him onto that lake where the ice is starting to melt.

Suddenly, there's the heart-stopping sound of splintering ice...

Both Jafet and Weirwolf fall into the water.

We stare, open-mouthed.

No one knows what to do. All we can think is that we must get Jafet out before he freezes and drowns.

Fortunately, the Weirwolf's extra size and weight drag him right down.

Jafet's luck is that he's so small and light he manages to bob up out of the water and hold his head above the ice.

We pull him out as quickly as possible. Though Jafet's nanosuit dries off immediately, his face, hands and feet are blue. His teeth chatter so hard, I'm convinced they might break. We rub him all over. We keep massaging his limbs until they go back to their normal healthy pink.

All this time Charlie doesn't take his eyes off that hole in the ice in case the Weirwolf reappears. 'Most dogs and wolves can swim,' he keeps reminding us.

But when there's no sign of the Weirwolf, he sighs and says, 'Come on. Let's keep walking.'

We do.

However, uppermost in our minds is, what if we meet more monsters?

What'll we do then? But no one says anything. Instead we gather everything together and continue following the shore of this lake.

19

The Village of Krodin

The weather starts to grow warmer. The snow melts in earnest. Soon we're sloshing through muddy puddles. No more ice. The lake turns a greyish-green.

Water trickles down a cliff and turns into waterfalls. Soon those waterfalls swell into raging torrents.

Icy fingers no longer pinch our faces, fingers and toes.

Much to Charlie and Rio's amazement we're coming into spring.

Rio whispers to me, though I don't understand why she must whisper, 'I'll never get used to all these changes.'

I nod. What can I say to make her feel better? Maybe one has to be used to moving between holos to know not to get upset.

Gradually, the sun gains more heat. Those grey lowering

clouds vanish leaving a lovely blue sky sprinkled with fluffy white clouds. Brown cliff-sides are flecked with green and purple bushes. These bushes sprout buds that unfurl into flowers. A light breeze rustles my hair. Birds sing. Bees hum. Cicadas trill. The day turns golden and green.

'It's like... as if we've walked into summer,' Rio murmurs.

The rest of us only gape at this much beauty.

A little further, the cliffs gradually level out and we're traversing a narrow pebble path flanked by tall elms that turns and leads into the countryside. We pass grassy paddocks divided by low stone walls. In the centre of each paddock is a round haystack topped with a steeple. Scattered amongst the grass are red flowers with long stems.

Rio stops to pick one. 'Poppies,' she says pointing to the central whirl of stamens. 'I'm sure these flowers are poppies.'

A little farther we come to train- rails that wind around a grassy hill and disappear into the distance.

We look at each other with raised eyebrows. What now?

Trist makes up our minds. 'Might as well follow them.'

On the other side of the hill we come to a small timber and red roof building. Rio murmurs, 'Guess that must be the station.'

Hoping to find a name or some hint that will tell us where we are, we walk inside. There are no people, no sign of where we might be, and the room is empty except for a cupboard on one wall with frosted glass doors.

'No-Name Station,' Charlie says and laughs. Since conquering Weirwolf, the twins no longer seem *quite* as upset by these rapid changes, at least not as much as they were to start with.

While we stand there wondering what to do next, Trist opens the cupboard. Inside he finds six bottles containing a clear beige fluid. 'Anyone game to try?'

'No way,' Zumi whines. 'What if it's poison?'

Rio opens one bottle and sniffs. 'Smells okay to me.' She takes a big sip. Then she half empties the bottle before saying, 'Fresh apple juice. Delicious.'

She drinks the rest. We watch her intensely. When nothing bad happens, we pass the other bottles around. Rio is right. That juice is not only delicious it gives an unexpected burst of strength.

Just then we hear something chugging down the track. We race outside. A small engine heading our way sends up clouds of steam. It reminds me of the train we caught way back when we could only travel via our avatars.

The train stops, waits for us to climb on and then takes off. We just have time to empty our bottles before we come to another station identical to the last, only this time the roof is green. Again no one is inside. Nor does this station have a name.

We walk through to the other side of the station and come into a village. I feel a sudden rush of joy. I know this village. This is where we come to meditate. But as we wander into the main street, I realise my mistake. These streets are narrower, there aren't as many trees, and the houses are cluttered messily together. Also, a hurricane must have recently passed through as whole buildings have collapsed, roofs lifted, and fallen walls show rooms where debris is strewn around like a giant child has thrown a tantrum.

As we walk through the village, it seems deserted. We wander through narrow streets looking for some sign of life. There's nothing. Not even a stray dog, cat, or chicken. Then the sky clouds over and we hear distant rumbling. The thunder grows louder. Lightning flashes. Two minutes later the clouds open. The wind rises. Heavy drops begin to fall. Within seconds, rain is pelting down in sheets.

'Must find shelter,' Rio gasps through a wind so fierce it almost prevents us from moving. As the wind rises to a high pitched howl, we push against it to follow Rio into a building that might once have been the village store. Here the roof has also been torn off, and the shelves are broken and empty. Charlie races through the building signalling for us to follow. By now the wind is too loud and strong to hear what anyone says.

'Hang on to each other,' Rio mouths, as on the other side we splash through muddy puddles fighting against that fierce gale to where Charlie has found a shed which still has a roof.

As we stand there dripping and shivering, wet hair plastered across our faces, Zumi notices the large round wooden-cover set into the floor.. Charlie reaches down and grabs the handle. Followed by a rush of water, the cover slides easily away exposing what looks like an underground entrance.

Outside the storm grows worse. Now the wind is so loud our ears throb with so much noise. Later Rio tells us that it sounded like a copter was overhead.

I see Charlie's mouth move, but the wind whips his words away. All I hear is '...shelter...'

We follow him into that dark entrance. Water pours in after us and it takes our combined strength to close the cover. We stand there awhile trying to make out where we are. I worry that there might be snakes or spiders. Though there are no lights, when we feel around, this narrow space extends to a tunnel. Down here the worst of the wind's howl might be cut out, but our surroundings are pitch-black. We can only feel our way by touching rough walls on both sides trying not to trip and fall. A draft twists around my ankles. It seems determined to pull me back. All I hear are footsteps as the others make their way along the tunnel. Where does it lead?

When something like a moth's feathery wings brushes against my cheeks, my heart gallops in fright.

Suddenly a light turns on.

Our eyes blink and water in the sudden glare.

A voice, a grown masc's voice, calls, 'Who are you? What are you doing in our village?'

Blinded by that bright light, no one knows what to say. Eventually Jafet pipes up, 'We're lost and looking for shelter. Can you please tell us where we are?'

More lanterns are turned on. We now see that we're standing in front of a group of about fifty adults and children. These people remind me of holos I've viewed of *Medieval Times*. They're all in battered fringed leather jerkins, thigh high boots, tight hose, and peaked hats.

The masc who challenged us, steps forward. He's got white hair, sad eyes, and a nose like a squashed tomato. What's not hidden of his face by a huge grey beard is as round and pink as an apple.

'This is the village of Krodin,' he tells us. 'Our families,' pointing to the people behind him, 'have lived here for countless generations.' His gaze wary, he pauses to look us over. When he understands that he's staring at six very wet youngsters, he evidently decides we must be harmless. 'Where are you from?'

Charlie says cautiously, 'We've come a very long way.' Then, 'What's been happening here?'

The masc shakes his head and gestures at his friends. They hide their faces in their hands and I hear the heart wrenching sound of people weeping. Only now do we see that there are only mascs. No fems. Rio asks, 'Where are your women?'

Tears run into the masc's cheeks into his beard. 'My name is Arturo and I am the village Elder. You want to know where our women are?' He gives a giant sigh. 'The monster Arachnida has kidnapped all our wives and daughters. We don't know what is happening to them, but we fear the very worst.'

We Hatchlings glance at each other. Zumi utters a little cry. She sinks onto her haunches and bursts into tears. I rush to hug and comfort her.

Rio stares wide-eyed at Zumi then turns to me. 'Who is Arachnida?'

Though we three Hatchlings are trembling almost as much as Zumi, Jafet manages to explain, 'Arachnida was one of our most challenging opponents in an endgame.'

'Yes.' I give a giant shudder. 'If it turns out that she is real, then she's totally terrifying.'

Charlie rests his hand on my shoulder. 'How terrifying? What exactly is she?'

'Arachnida is a gargantuan spider,' I tell him.

'How big?' Rio asks.

'Bigger than this room,' I half sob. 'And unbelievably powerful.'

Charlie frowns and turns back to Arturo. 'Isn't there some way to get your women back?'

Arturo shakes his head. 'Don't think we haven't tried. You saw our village?' We all nod. 'That is what happens if anyone annoys Arachnida. She is destruction itself.'

'Can't you stop her?' Charlie asks.

Arturo's beard trembles, 'There is a prophecy that says she can only be beaten by young females who are brave enough to plunge a sword into her heart. So far no one has ever managed to get close enough. Now all our women are in her hands. Perhaps your girls can help us?'

At this, we can only gulp. If all these grown-ups are helpless, what can three young fems do?'

As if he guesses our thoughts, another masc steps forward. He wears a short dark beard and is younger than Arturo. 'Before you take this on,' he tells us, 'we must warn you that Arachnida's children will do everything they can to distract you. Never think fighting them will be easy.'

By now everyone has settled in a circle on the floor. The villagers demand to know our names and ages. This time we tell them the truth. They seem astonished to hear that we Hatchlings are the same age as the twins, but then put it down to our mother's misfortune. 'No one woman should carry four babies,' Arturo grunts. 'No wonder you youngsters are so small.'

We glance at each other. Though as far as we know, no woman gave birth to us, perhaps he's right in us being unfortunate.

Eventually Arturo says, 'We villagers have learnt to be careful of strangers. Therefore we would like to know what brought you here.'

We tell him about running away from the Snouts, living with The Children and finding ourselves in the icy landscape, but not about the contents of the cave. Then conquering Weirwolf, how the weather inexplicably changed, and the train that brought us here.

If the villagers find all this too amazing, they give no hint of this. Instead they talk for a long while amongst themselves before Arturo turns to us to say, 'If you managed to conquer the Weirwolf, you may be the help we seek.'

We glance at the crowd who nod like one person.

'But... but we don't know anything about her,' Charlie bravely tells them. 'You will need to fill us in.'

At this, a masc calls, 'Our ancestors tell us that Arachnida has always lived close by, but that she was in a thousand year sleep. Unfortunately her sleep ended not long ago.'

'What happened then?' Charlie asks.

'She became increasingly jealous of other women. She hates competition of any kind and enjoys using her amazing powers.'

Trist asks, 'What are they?'

'She is able to create amazing hurricanes that tear our buildings down and capture our women. She's kidnapped our wives and daughters, and hidden them we think in her castle.'

There's a long silence.

Finally Rio asks in a very small voice, 'What has she done with them?'

Arturo takes a long time to answer this. 'We don't know.' Tears roll down his apple-pink cheeks. 'Arachnida is totally unpredictable. She may already have eaten them.'

We three fems glance nervously at each other. If Arachnida knows that we're here, won't she try to kidnap us as well?

'Isn't there anything you can tell us that might help?' Jafet asks.

The villagers go into a huddle. When they come out of it, Arturo says, 'Our only weapon was to attempt to confuse Arachnida. We told her that there is a prophecy that only two young girls can overcome her power and that they must be born in Krodin.'

'Is that true? I ask.

He gives me a small smile. 'Only partially. It's true that the prophecy says young girls will finally overcome her. But not that they must be born in Krodin.'

Meanwhile the other mascs are busy setting up chairs and a table. They lay out platters of bread, cheese, tomatoes, and jugs of frothy apple juice. Arturo points us to some chairs and invites us to eat. Hungry, we don't wait to be asked. No one says much. The villagers are too miserable to talk and we're too scared. But I do notice that the adult mascs drink a different kind of apple-juice they call 'cider'. After they have filled, drunk and emptied several mugs, they become far more cheerful.

When all the food disappears, someone starts to sing. Soon everyone takes up this song. The music is slow and sad. Tears start to my eyes as they sing,

Love has no season or
reason or rhyme
But is here forever
to keep us sublime...

There's lots more verses. But by this time the mascs have drunk so much cider, the words run into each other and I can't understand them.

When we finish eating, the table is cleared, blankets are placed on the floor, and the villagers settle down to sleep.

But before we do the same, Arturo beckons Rio, Zumi and me into a corner where we won't be overheard. There, he gives each of us a dagger covered in a leather sheath. 'Hide this in your clothes,' he tells us. 'And always remember... if Arachnida attacks you, that she can only be conquered by thrusting a dagger into her chest in the hope that you penetrate her heart. Can you remember this?'

We gulp and nod.

20

Arachnida

At first I must sleep very soundly, because I wake only when, still asleep, I try to turn over. When I find I can't move, I try to sit up...

Only then do I realise that I can't shift in any direction.

I'm trapped!

Somehow during the night, my hands and feet have been tied together and now I'm stuck.

My shrill cry wakes the others.

Trist jumps to his feet. Arturo, who has not drunk as much cider as the other villagers, rushes over to me. 'What's wrong?' He turns on his lamp. I now see that my arms and legs have been bound with sticky grey strands. Whatever these strands touch, they cling with an iron grip. All I can do is turn my neck, and then only to see that Zumi and Rio have also been captured.

From Arturo's horrified face, I know this is Arachnida's doing. She's caught us fems and she intends taking us to the same place she took the fem villagers. But what if they're no longer alive? What if she intends to kill us with her lethal bite and then place our bodies in her larder? In my Arachnida endgame, Henny always made sure I would emerge victorious.

But this isn't a Virtual endgame Henny is controlling.

This Arachnida actually exists.

The mascs do their best to try and untie us, but their efforts are useless. Those sticky ropes only find more places to attach themselves. Then we hear a strange stamping noise, the sound of many feet, as if an army is marching our way. Dark crab-like creatures emerge from the shadows. Scores of spiders surround me. They are big as butter plates and their hairy legs touch me all over. The sweet sick-making odour of rotting meat makes me want to throw up. I struggle against their cords. But it's useless. There's nothing I can do. I'm well and truly caught.

All Arturo has time to yell before we're carried away, is 'Remember to use your daggers.'

Next, the spiders are carrying us along a narrow pitch-black tunnel. Sometimes they scrape my arms and legs against the walls. Soon I'm covered in scratches and bruises. The tunnel takes a right hand turn. Then another. And another. This last leads directly into a cave where a huge wooden door is set into the far wall. The spiders dump us on the floor and leave us there.

Tears roll down our cheeks. What will happen to us now? What if we're kept here forever? Tied up like this without water and food we'll never survive.

We're left there for what seems like hours. How I wish I was back in my Cell with Tutor-Henny. I never did appreciate how much she did for me. How comfortable my life was. Though living in a Cell with only an avatar to show me the world left lots to be desired, waiting for a spider to eat me is surely worse.

Some of my thoughts must seep through to the others because Zumi can't stop sobbing. After a while Rio gets angry enough to yell, 'Zumi, if you don't stop crying, I'll... I'll...' She's left speechless. But tied up like this, all threats seem stupid.

I feel I should try and defend Zumi. 'Rio, don't get cross. She's just scared.'

'We're all scared,' Rio says tightly. 'You're scared. I'm scared too. But crying isn't going to help. We need to think of ways to overcome her, ways to use our daggers.'

But the small dagger strapped to my thigh feels so useless, I just shudder. Tears roll down my cheeks. I can't even move my hands to wipe them away.

We wait and wait. Do the spiders intend leaving us here forever?

But it seems Arachnida has other plans for us. Eventually the spiders return. One scuttles up the door to peer inside a peephole. He communicates to someone on the other side.

At this, the door slowly swings opens and we're staring into an enormous hall where distant walls and ceilings are festooned with a soft grey fabric spun from silk.

We're carried into the hall. It's very dim in here. What little light there is comes from the other side of the hangings. Down the very far end up on a dais is a figure as large as a building. The spiders rush us towards her. We're dumped in front of a monstrous spider seated on a throne-like chair with ornate carvings.

Not that we can tell what Arachnida's body looks like because she's covered in a loose gown the same horrid grey as the walls. This gown moves and billows as if it's covering a hundred hidden legs. But we don't take much notice of her body. It's her face that rivets our gaze. That spider's face is so expressionless I could never imagine anything this terrifying. Not even in my worst nightmare.

Back in our Cells both Zumi and I had several times overcome Arachnida's clever wiles by having our avatars use their swords and spears to pierce her heart. But those had been played out in an endgame where our avatars were able to leap over monsters the size of buildings, and perform amazing acrobatics. This time both Arachnida and her spiders are real. This time we don't own any swords. Nor are we able to perform amazing acrobatics. This time we have to rely on mere cleverness.

Arachnida's skin is the palest of pale grey. Only her huge black eyes and cruel thin lips distinguish her from the wall hangings. Yet that gaze manages to hold us in thrall. It seems to reduce everything she looks at into nothing.

For a long time no one says anything. Then Arachnida addresses Rio. 'Why are you here... here..?' Her voice is human, high, almost a squeak, but it echoes and reverberates around her chamber.

Rio opens her mouth.

Nothing comes out.

Arachnida turns her attention to me and Zumi. 'Why are you here... here... here?'

We're also too frightened to speak.

Arachnida shifts impatiently. At this, several spiders scuttle towards her. They carry a mug filled with some dark bubbling liquid and climb tall ladders to reach her mouth.

She ignores her children and what they are bringing her.

Again she says, 'Why did you decide to come to Krodin... din.. din... din? The echo grows louder though interspersed with odd cracklings.

At last Rio finds her voice. 'We didn't come here on purpose,' she says carefully.

'Speak up, child...ild...ild...' Arachnida irritably demands.

Rio gulps and tries again. 'We were lost,' she almost shouts. 'A train came along. We didn't know where it was going, but that train brought us here.'

'Ahhh..,' Arachnida considers this. She utters a sigh that can only be one of relief. 'Then the prophecy cannot come true... true...' as the echo continues, it seep into our very soul.

21

Overcoming her wiles

For a long moment I'm rigid with fear and too scared to think properly. I'm sure my eyes are starting out of my head Then it strikes me...isn't Arachnida talking about the same prophecy Arturo mentioned?

If so, didn't he give her wrong information?

I glance at the others. From their expressions I can tell they're equally terrified. But now all this fright forces my brain to start working. Hadn't Arturo told us that Arachnida only knows part of the true prophecy? Hadn't he mentioned that the only way to overcome Arachnida was to pierce her chest with our daggers? Didn't he also tell us that no one had ever got close enough to her to do this before? And that it must be done by a young fem? Shouldn't we make the most of Arachnida's belief in something that foretold her end if she thinks it can't be us?

I do my best to swallow my fear and yell as loudly as I can, 'Please Arachnida. We don't know anything about any prophecy. Will you tell us more about it?'

A gust of wind racing through her grey silken gown makes it swell, billow, and then deflate. I shudder and try not to picture how many hundreds of arms and legs must be hidden under that gown.

She muses a moment, then says, 'It is said that my power can be overcome only by women and girls who were born in Krodin....din...din...'

There was still that strange echo effect interspersed with crackling, but there's no time to wonder at it...

'That is why I kidnapped all the village women. However, as you have come from Outside, I would doubt that you have any power over me or that you can make this prophecy come true... ue...'

Fortunately, Rio has the presence of mind to ask, 'Where do you get all your power?'

'How can you ask such a question?' Arachnida asks indignantly. 'Don't you know that I own all the power in this valley... ey.. ey...?

Her voice seems to seep into our brains. Another shiver runs down my spine. How can anyone ever even attempt to overcome such a monster?

There are more strange echoes and grumbling crackling sounds before she adds, 'Wasn't I able to produce hurricanes, tempests and storms that destroyed all the village buildings and brought the owners to heel... eel... eel?'

We look at each other and shake our heads. I yell, 'Why should we believe you?'

Her laugh is scornful. 'I will prove it to you by turning it off and on...on...on...'

Her room goes pitch black. Then that same dim light comes back on. But as she turns the power off and on, something goes wrong. There are more curious noises.

Has she created another storm?

Can she bring it into this room?

I can't think what that noise can be until Rio whispers. 'Know what? It sounds like an amplifier gone wrong.'

'What's an amplifier?' I whisper back.

'Amplifiers magnify sound. They make sure everyone can hear what's being said.'

Now Arachnida addresses us. But for some reason her voice is suddenly so soft, we can see her lips move, but can't hear what she's saying. Also, that strange echo has disappeared.

Rio shouts, 'We can't hear what you're saying.'

Arachnida frowns and gestures to her spiders to bring us towards her.

'No,' Rio yells. 'We still can't hear. If you want us to know what you're saying, you have to untie us.'

Arachnida signals to her spiderlings to do just that.

After being tied up for so long, we suffer terrible pins and needles. We have to rub our arms and jump up and down to get any blood back into our limbs.

Arachnida beckons us towards her. Then she says in that faint squeaky tone, 'My voice is tired. If you still want to know what the prophecy foretold you must come even closer.'

We do. Now we're only a few paces away, we have to tilt our heads right back so we can look up at her.

Rio takes advantage of this. She calls, 'We still can't hear you.'

We take a few more steps towards Arachnida.

We watch her mouth open and close.

'We still can't hear,' Rio yells.

'Then you must come even closer.'

'Watch out, it's a trap,' Zumi yells just as Arachnida's mouth gapes open. Rio uses that moment to wave her dagger up at the giant spider's face. While Arachnida is trying to see what Rio is up to, Zumi and I rush forward to plunge our daggers into her body.

There's a terrific gust of air, and a loud explosion as Arachnida's body deflates and falls onto the floor. A mask with a spring-mouth pivots and falls. Under the mask is a pile of scaffolding. We suddenly wake up that this Arachnida, a monster able to frighten an entire village and kidnap all its women, was mostly composed of a giant balloon and a face-mask manipulated from inside. As we watch that grey robe and mask fall onto the floor, a microphone tumbles after it.

Arachnida wriggles out from under.

Turns out that that this spider is the same size as a very large dinner plate.

No wonder her voice was soft.

No wonder she had to use an amplifier to confuse her victims.

With one movement, Rio jumps on her. There's a squeak of protest, then a sickening gut-hollowing squelch. Just to makes sure she's quite dead, I plunge my dagger into her corpse. That's the end of Arachnida. When her spiderlings see what has happened, those cowards scuttle away.

Now all that's left for us is to find what the spiders have done with the Krodin fems.

It's Zumi who thinks to look behind the grey hangings that surround that vast room. Sure enough, there are doors behind it that lead into a long corridor flanked by many rooms. We look inside every one. Most are empty, though we do find some remains in one that might once have been human. Our hearts sink. Is this what has happened to the Krodin fems?

Then Rio flings open the door to the last room. And there they are; both old and young. Huddled together, those fems are almost paralyzed by terror. When they realise we are there to rescue them, it's a pleasure to view their relief and joy.

'We thought you were the spiders come to fetch us as food for Arachnida and her children,' the oldest fem tells us. Turns out she is Arturo's wife and when we finally crawl through the spiders' tunnels back to the cave where the mascs are waiting, their rejoicing is enormous.

But there is still something we don't understand.

Much later Jafet asks Arturo, 'How did Arachnida manage to tear down all those buildings?'

He scratches his beard before answering. 'Because she owns all the power in this valley, she built an incredibly powerful storm machine. She also used that machine to make herself seem so much bigger and scare us into giving her anything she wants.'

'Was that prophecy true?'

There's a glimmer of a smile behind that bushy beard. 'It's said that she can only be overcome by two girls that are small for their age. I think Pya and Zumi must be the youngsters this refers to.'

The celebrations continue far into the night. The villagers are so grateful for our help they set about preparing a wonderful feast. As well as the cheese and bread we ate on our first night, the villagers produce their favourite foods: chocolate and strawberry milkshakes, toast covered in grilled tomato and cheese, delicious three tiered sandwiches and fruit pies. And the very best chocolate cake, cheese-cake, shortbread topped with strawberry jam, and doughnuts sprinkled with cinnamon and sugar. As well, they have every possible dish that can be made with apples: apple cake, apple dumplings, apple muffins, baked apples with cinnamon, apple and prune compote, and of course, lots of apple juice.

This time all the villagers also drink a great deal of cider, but this time their songs are happy. They sing:

Love has no season or
reason or rhyme
But is here forever
to keep us sublime.

The celebrations last almost all night. In the end we're too tired to stay awake, but we're lulled to sleep by the villagers' new song.

Next morning that we wake to a vastly different scene.

PART 5.

CYBERTRICKS

22

Galaxian Endgame

During the night, and without knowing anything about it, we've been moved to a desert of yellow sand and orange rock.

We sit up.

Our mouths drop open and our jaws gape as we stare around.

What we see is totally desolate: no trees, no bushes, no grass. Nothing moves. Only brown hills that seem to roll on forever, a weird yellow-green sky, and a giant orange sun half dipping below the horizon.

I gasp aloud. Isn't this my old nightmare come to life? Isn't this the terrifying landscape I dreamt about before we were first thrown back to this century?

Does this mean we're about to meet that same monster?

I turn to Rio and Charlie. Uppermost in my mind is; how will they cope with another change? Before I have time to find out, Zumi points towards the hills. Two tractors are chugging towards us. They stop just in front. We get up close enough to look inside. Both tractors are driverless. However, one carries a container labelled 'food'. The other has bottles labelled 'water'.

It's already so hot, sand burns our feet, and the air feels like the inside of an oven. I can hardly breathe.

'Don't touch those bottles,' Charlie warns through cracked lips. 'They could make us sick.'

Trist pulls one out.

Charlie tries to stop him. 'What if it's a trap?'

Too late. Trist has already opened the bottle and drunk from it. 'Tastes fine,' he manages between gulps. We crouch in the tractors' shadows and wait. When nothing bad happens, we also drink. Never has water tasted this good. The other tractor is filled with boxes of sandwiches containing delicious fillings.

We finish everything.

What now? It doesn't take long to find out. We nearly jump out of our skins when an unseen voice calls, 'Welcome new contestants… welcome. Please climb in and we will take you to your quarters.'

What will happen if we don't?

We look at the tractors, then at each other. But surrounded by a waterless desert, with no shelter food or water, we can only obey.

Once we've all climbed in, those tractors carry us towards those brown hills and over the other side. In the middle of a flat plain is a large square building. The tractors move towards it. Up close this building is huge.

'Almost as big as a shopping mall,' Rio murmurs.

A sign reads:

**Welcome to the
Galaxian Endgame Festival.**

**Watch the most terrifying creature
in the universe take on all comers.**

Half price tickets for two or more games.

We reach a door on the far side of the building. Both tractors come to a halt.

'This is where you will stay until it's your turn to join us,' the unseen speaker informs us.

But all this time I can't forget that nightmare. Did it come from playing too many endgames? Or is it a warning?

In that dream I remember hurtling into an unknown galaxy where a billion suns almost blinded me. I remember plummeting through space until landing on the fourth moon of a planet into a desert of yellow sand and brown hills. I remember that giant orange sun dipping below the horizon, only endless dunes stretching as far as the eye can see. Just as in my dream, a low wind builds up speed and whips around us. Dust-devils spiral. As we stand there desperate to escape, blood pounding in our ears, our hearts in our mouths, somehow I know something dreadful is about to happen ... something mind-blowing and horrid!

Seems Jafet also had that dream. He also understands this is similar to some of the endgames we played back in our Cells because he says in a small voice, 'Isn't this like when we had to fight the Shape-Shifter?'

Trist bites his lower lip. 'That loudspeaker did call us "contestants".'

'And that sign did welcome us to the Galaxian Endgame Festival,' I slowly add.

As such a possibility hits the others, Zumi stares at Jafet, then at me in horror. 'You're saying…' her voice rises, '…you're saying that we might have to fight a Shape-Shifter? An actual Shape-Shifter?'

I stare stonily back. 'Didn't we have to fight Weirwolf and Arachnida? Weren't they also endgames we played back in our Cells?'

Rio gulps. I'm sure she's never been this frightened. Not even when the Snouts or those other monsters threatened to devour us. In a trembling voice, she asks, 'Wh…what are Shape-Shifters.'

All we Hatchlings can do is stare blankly back. My stomach churns. Zumi hides her face in her hands. Trist gave a hopeless shrug. Only Jafet can find words to explain, 'Shape-Shifters are exactly what their name suggests. They're the most frightening creatures in the universe because they're almost impossible to catch or to fight. Each time you think you've beaten or captured a Shape-Shifter it morphs into something else.'

Just to make sure we know this is correct, there's a blare of music, a long drum-roll, and a high-pitched voice cries, 'Sentient Beings of the Galaxy, welcome to the Ten Thousandth Universal Game where constant streams of fresh contestants are pitted against the famous Betelgeux Shape-Shifter!'

There's a roar of applause.

We're being watched. Of course, we're being watched by an unseen audience. No wonder we're alone. No one with any sense would come to a planet where a Shape-Shifter roams freely. I'm sure we're on display in a billion holos right now. I also suspect that this vast unseen audience fully expects us to succumb to the Shape-Shifter.

We climb out of the tractors and walk into a carpeted area furnished with tables, chairs, sofas and couches. In here, the air is cool and sweet. Behind this room, a passage feeds into other rooms with luxurious sleep and bath-pods. No sentient beings. Not anywhere. Not even any robots. I'm totally terrified. But the major difference between the endgame we played in our Cells is that back then I was alone or partnering Zumi. This time we are six.

If we think we're the very next contestants, this isn't so. We're left in that building for two more days and nights. Trolleys wheel in at regular intervals with interesting drinks and delicious foods. Floors are lined with colourful carpets. Bathroom taps gush water. Beds couldn't be more comfortable. There are lots of interesting holos to watch. An open courtyard in the centre of the building has a huge swimming pool with the bluest water imaginable. Other places are set aside where we can play. Whoever is holding us captive has no intention of letting us get thirsty, hungry, tired, or bored, and thus avoid becoming part of their spectacle. The contrast to trekking through the bush, to living with The Children, to fighting the Weirwolf in a frozen landscape, and to arriving in the medieval village of Krodin with Arachnida's terrifying underground palace, couldn't be more marked.

If only we were allowed to enjoy it. But every so often, the unseen speaker announces more rules. 'All contestants are allowed to bring anything they own to help them fight our Shape-Shifter.'

Each announcement is met with a roar of applause.

'Contestants have exactly ten Terran minutes to beat the Shape-Shifter. However, if before that time is up they can manage to bluff him into submission, the contest ends there.'

More roars.

More applause.

More terror.

Every time there's another announcement, we shake in our shoes. What we should do is share every bit of information we know about Shape-Shifters. Mostly, we're too scared even to begin. We sit around hoping for all this to go away, for *ComCen* to rescue us. 'What hope do we have?' Jafet dismally pronounces. 'Nothing and no-one has ever succeeded in destroying a Shape-Shifter. They are universally known to be invincible. No one has ever managed to combat its ability to change and morph into other beings...'

He goes on and on...

He never stops.

By now the twins' cheeks are permanently grey.

'Shut up Jafet,' I fiercely whisper. 'Scaring everyone isn't going to help.'

He stares at me helpless in his own flow. His face crumples. 'Surely it's wisest to know the worst things about them. It must help for us to go over every bit of information we can gather.'

Charlie gulps. 'How do you know what they're like?'

'Back in our cells when we played endgame, it was the only creature we never could beat. That right, Trist?'

'Yes.' Trist's face is sombre. 'Shape-Shifters are unbeatable.'

What if we refuse to believe this?

I yell, 'You're just giving up before we've even started. We have to think positive.'

Jafet sighs and nods. 'Pya's right. We must work out some

way to hold it off.'

By now Trist is strong enough to complete a headstand. These days all four hatchlings seem taller and stronger.

We wait for Trist to cartwheel back onto his feet before asking, 'Anyone got an idea?'

To our astonishment Zumi, who until now never speaks except to sob and moan and complain, says, 'First us Hatchlings need to make a list of everything we know or ever heard about Shape-Shifters.'

We blink and stare. 'Good on you Zumi,' Trist finally murmurs. 'Okay with you, Pya, Jafet?'

We both nod.

Zumi looks pleased. 'Okay, what exactly do we know?'

I say, 'A Shape-Shifter can morph into any creature or spirit depending on who it is fighting.'

Everyone falls silent. Eventually Charlie murmurs, 'What hope do we have? We don't even have a laser.'

Jafet laughs sourly. 'Any known weapon is useless against a Shape-Shifter.'

No one says anything.

No one knows what to say.

I'm convinced *ComCen* brought us here. But why? If *She's* still partially operational it must have something to do with this exercise about coming together as a team. I mention this to the others and from then on we talk and talk. No one argues. None of us dare waste precious time and energy squabbling about petty matters. This is a matter of life or death.

Instead we look for anything that might give some protection. All we have are tables, chairs, crockery, cutlery, bath-pods and sleep-pods. Can any of these be turned into weapons? We spend a long time discussing this. Can chairs be used as shields? Broken plates and knives become swords? If we arm ourselves we might manage to confuse the Shape-Shifter long enough to hold out for that token ten minutes.

At first we can't see how we can carry this through. How can household goods be used against the scariest creature in the known universe? Only after we spend more time figuring it out, does everyone take on this idea. Anyway, we have no choice.

23

Fighting the Shape-Shifter

What we finally do agree on is that this can't work unless we stay together. We have to act as one. Five of us will use chairs as shields. This, plus Trist turning cartwheels, we can with luck, confuse the Shape-Shifter into dropping his guard long enough for the time we're given to hold out against him.

Right now ten minutes seems more like ten hours, ten days, ten years, ten millennia.

It's Zumi who insists that we bring bed-sheets as well. Though we can't see how these can help, for once no one argues. No one has the energy or will to disagree. This is far too fraught. Though no one says it aloud, I'm sure none of us think we can hold out long enough to survive.

Nothing happens until half way through our third day when a distant roar tells us a Shape-Shifter is on its way. Sure enough, we go outside and see far off the outline of a giant reptile, a creature that never walked on Terra.

We arrange ourselves in a semicircle and wait for the Shape-Shifter to stride towards us. The creature comes close enough to tower like a six-story building. Its body, front legs, head and scaly skin are like a giant reptile's. From out of its mouth countless snakes with forked tongues aim at us.

It's as if a wind rushes through my ears. Maybe there are roars and cheers from that unseen audience, but I don't hear anything. My mouth is too dry. Every limb feels limp. Powerless. I'm sure we can never beat it.

I know it's stupid even to try.

Liquid trickles down my legs.

If only I could stop trembling... how can I even attempt to think clearly when I'm so frightened? This creature is truly dreadful. Those writhing snakes make him even scarier. I'm sure there's no way we can overcome it. A real monster is far more terrifying than any nightmare. Gazing up at it, I can't believe we'll even manage to hold out long enough for that shape-shifter to morph into another shape.

Trembling, shivering with such fear as we wait for the inevitable, I hear Jafet yell, 'Hold up your chairs!'

I manage to follow his order. Just. So do the others. The creature peers down at these cheeky creatures. I swear an incredulous glimmer appears in those inflamed eyes. Who are these puny humans daring to confront him? He opens his mouth. A giant roar emerges. Brown saliva drips onto us. Snake heads dart forked tongues our way. But even if we manage to hold this reptile off, can't a Shape-Shifter morph into any shape it desires?

No way can we beat it through any fair fight. I think back to Weirwolf and Arachnida. When we met them in reality, we six coming together did overthrow them. But what did help was using what we had learnt in our endgame and more importantly, about cooperating as a team. In comparison those monsters were nothing compared to trying to overcome a Shape-Shifter. Can we succeed without using our old avatars? Can we do this without *ComCen*'s help? What makes things harder is that we won't have Rio and Charlie's help. Neither twin has ever experienced what it's like to fight a Shape-Shifter.

No time to ask questions.

'Remember the endgame,' I remind the other three Hatchlings as the reptile's mouth opens wider and the forked snake tongues come closer. 'Think yourself into T-Rex.'

I concentrate hard. Sure enough, and to my own amazement, I feel myself grow and grow. I feel myself expand into the equally terrifying T-Rex. Behind me so do three other Hatchlings. The Shape-Shifter's reddish eyes narrow. The creature takes one step back. There's a slight pause before it morphs into the largest and most ferocious tiger anyone can imagine. His growl is loud enough to echo around the hills.

But now the others know what to do. Trist yells, 'Everyone…think lion,' and all together we four morph into lions even bigger than the Shape-Shifter.

Confronted by equally ferocious creatures, and briefly out-flanked, the Shape-Shifter morphs into a giant bat. Our answer is to transform our lions into ferocious wolves.

Then the Shape-Shifter changes into a giant spider crab with arms that fire like cannons.

We respond by turning into giant bears with glinting metal teeth like those worn by the Snout fem, Fobia.

It responds by becoming a giant crab.

All this time an unseen audience screams hysterically If those viewers had thought this game sewn up, the contest is turning into something different. But just in case we think we've won, the Shape-Shifter has one more trick up its sleeve.

It dissolves into something amorphous, something almost impossible to track down. It turns into a shadow. Though we have only one minute for the game to be over, we have no defence against something formless. I feel a huge wave of despair. If the shadow catches us, this is endgame in reality and the Shape-Shifter has won.

Fortunately, Zumi thinks to yell, 'Sheets! Trap it inside.'

The idea is to form a circle and try to surround the shadow with these bed-sheets and trap the Shape-Shifter inside. This time Rio and Charlie join in. Though it looks as if the Shape-Shifter must surely win as it dodges and ducks between six enormous sheets that fill out like giant balloons, it makes a serious mistake by heading straight for Trist.

Trist is quick enough to handspring away. This confuses the Shape-Shifter. We can only assume that it has never come across this action before. It loses an important moment. Only a tiny flicker. But that's long enough for three Hatchlings to turn into our final avatar known as Gigantica Humanoidus, giants that can circle any shadow and entangle him inside our sheets.

A buzzer sounds.

A roar goes up. The roar is followed by tumultuous applause.

That buzzer means we've beaten the Shape-Shifter.

As the clapping grows louder, the unseen voice rises to call, 'The Shape-Shifter has lost. As your reward, you can return to the planet of your choice…'

I know a momentary blackness.
And then?
Nothing.

24

Back on Terra

I open my eyes to the same giddiness as when I first moved back into real body and I was no longer in my avatar. I know a long time has passed because I'm both hungry and thirsty. I know I slept and slept because I dreamt that I was back in Cell Q3, my old home. Only this time the Cell is deserted. My sleep-pod unmade. My food-tubes empty.

Where is Tutor-Henny?

Why isn't *She* here?

Tears trickle down my cheeks. I open my eyes and look straight into a furry face. I start up, my heart about to jump out of my chest.

Only then do I recognise this face as belonging to a dog. We're back on Terra, lying on green grass beside a haystack surrounded by purplish hills. In the distance I hear sounds I finally recognise as surf washing onto a beach.

But right then our attention is taken up by that dog. He has sharp pointy gleaming teeth and a very pink tongue. A man is with him.

Charlie and Trist scramble to their feet.

The dog barks wildly.

'Quiet, Roth,' says the man. The dog obeys. To my astonishment I recognise this stranger as the fat man from Slide Forever. I'd know that grey hair, red nose, red cheeks and big belly anywhere. Too frightened to wonder at yet another coincidence, I watch Charlie go to hit the dog. The dog barks and leaps at him. Before he can make contact, the man grabs Charlie's arm. 'Hold it, son.'

Charlie does.

They study each other. The man frowns. 'What are you youngsters doing here?'

Apparently Charlie decides that this man will never believe our story about any of our other adventures, and certainly not about beating a Shape-Shifter in a Galaxian Endgame festival. He says, 'We had to run away… there's Snouts and sickness back there.'

He pauses long enough to let the rest of us pick up the story. Rio says, 'We were living with The Children, only they got sick. Their little ones were dying…' his voice trails away.

Rio picks up our story '…and we got scared we might catch their sickness.'

'Ah,' says the man. 'Heard both those were around.' He looks us over. 'You lot hungry?'

After all the energy we used beating the Shape-Shifter, we suddenly realise we're starving.

The man considers this. He says, 'Don't be scared. I'm Bert. Me and the wife live over there.' He points to a house on top of the hill. 'Come on home, and we'll find you something to eat.'

We do. Instinct tells us this old man is kind, and we won't come to any harm. Roth leads us through two paddocks. Bert's fem, Nance, meets us by the kitchen door. She has fine wrinkly skin, white hair caught in a bun, pale blue eyes and uses a walking stick. I recognise her as the old woman I saw before I fell from Slide Forever.

'They've just escaped from the Snouts and The Children. They say The Children have some sickness,' Bert tells her. 'I reckon these kids might be hungry.'

'Poor things!' says Nance. 'We don't have much. But you're welcome to what we have.'

Almost in tears at this much generosity, we watch Nance place food on the table. A jug of milk. Bread. Butter. Hard boiled eggs. Tomatoes and apples. 'Tuck in,' says Bert. 'All home produce.'

We don't need any encouragement.

Bert waits for us to finish. 'Where are your parents?' he asked.

Tears start to Charlie's eyes. 'We don't know. We lost them leaving the city.'

'We heard what happened.' Bert's gaze flickers over us Hatchlings. 'And these younger uns...' he frowned slightly. 'Brothers and sisters?'

'Me and Rio, we're twins. And them...' Charlie decides it safest to stay consistent, 'Them... they're the quads.'

'Unusual but cute,' says Nance. 'How old are they?'

'Thirteen...' Rio kicks him under the table. 'Ah... six.'

What if Bert also views us 'devil spawn'?

What will we do then?

'Hmm,' says Nance. 'Hardly six. You quads look more like

you're ten or eleven.'

At this Jafet rushes in with, 'We're much older than we look. We're really...'

As he pauses uncertainly, I decide to tell the truth. 'We're the same ages as the twins. We're really thirteen.'

'Hmm, that's more like it,' Nance agrees. 'Just a bit short and undeveloped for your age.'

It's true we are aware that we are all growing very rapidly. In fact, our recent growth spurt has been remarkable.

'What with conditions in the City,' she adds. 'You probably never got enough to eat.'

Though this wasn't the case, I decide not to put her right.

'Listen.' Bert settles himself next to Charlie. 'You'll need somewhere to stay. I've a shed for you to sleep in and mattresses. In exchange, you can help out with some chores.'

'See how kind they are?' I whisper to Zumi as Bert and Roth shepherd us outside. 'Do you remember them from Slide Forever? They didn't have to feed us, did they? As I said before, they're not stupid. They're just old.'

Zumi shrugs. But I know she knows I'm right.

25

'Utopia'

That farm is wonderful. 'Utopian,' is Jafet's quick description. 'What does that mean?' I ask.

He shrugs. 'Just that everything is quite, quite perfect.'

It certainly is. Even if the rest of the country lacks proper drinking water, Bert had dug around until he found a natural spring that waters his animals and crops. He obtains his energy from the wind and the sun and from recycling leftovers. The farm is totally self-sufficient. What's more, when the first lawlessness broke out, Nance was wise enough to store many sacks of rice, sugar and flour and we help her bake bread and cakes. Living on that farm is wonderful. There were so many activities we enjoy... such as getting to know their dog Roth, and Bert giving us our very first riding lesson on his old mare, Hera.

'Hera, just like our tutor-holos,' I say to Zumi.

'A horse like a tutor?' She laughs. 'Pya, sometimes you're so weird.'

My eyes roll skyward. Then I gently explain, 'I mean they both start with the letter H.' I don't get mad anymore. I know she doesn't mean to hurt my feelings. This is just Zumi's way. Nor do I any longer get annoyed with the mascs. And on the odd occasion when I do, I know to walk away until I get over it.

Every evening before bedtime, the six of us get together to arrange the next day's timetable. We always make sure that every chore, both good and bad, are shared. No one is forced to do anything he or she can't manage. For example, Charlie often helps Trist and Jafet chop wood so that the kitchen stove never goes out. The mascs never allow Bert to carry anything heavy. A week later over the evening meal, Bert says, 'Don't know I managed this farm before you youn' uns turned up.'

Nance is so frail, and Rio so busy helping the mascs with farm jobs, Zumi and I take turns milking their cows and searching the chicken-coop for eggs. We thoroughly enjoy weeding, planting, and collecting fruit and vegetables. Though we put in very long hours, sunrise to sunset, no one minds. That's because we're doing things together. Sometimes when I think back to Cell Q3, I can hardly believe I'm that same person who could barely manage to crawl from sleep-pod to chair.

There is an old piano in their living room which, Nance assures me, is terribly out of tune. With Trist's help, we fix this instrument so I can use it to create music. Hidden inside a chair, I find tattered albums of what Nance tells me are famous classical pieces. I soon learn to follow what she calls 'notation'. Within weeks, I am playing Bach's 48 Preludes and Fugues. Several Mozart concerti, all the Scarlatti and Beethoven Sonatas, Chopin etudes and nocturnes, some Schubert and Schumann songs and just about everything Liszt ever wrote. Then I compose my own music.

Nance is certainly impressed. She says, 'Few great pianists ever mastered such a repertoire.'

I also play some of the simple folk songs Bert hums for me. 'Wonderful technique,' he tells me. 'But you need to put more emotion into what you play.'

I frown, puzzled.

'You need to play that music as if you are speaking about those feelings deep inside you,' he explains.

Though I try very hard to do this, at first it seems impossible. Only when he suggests that when I play, I recall some terrible loss, does his advice begin to make sense. So when I play, I think of how I may never see Tutor-Henny again. Or how sad I was when The Children's youngest hatchling died. Or how I felt when the Weirwolf tried to attack Charlie. Or how we felt when Arachnida and the Shape-Shifter nearly destroyed us.

The others group around me to listen. When I finish playing, tears run down the old couple's cheeks. 'Never thought I'd hear such magic again,' Nance murmurs. Bert holds her in his arms and they remain silent a very long time.

Meanwhile Zumi is using bits and pieces she finds scattered around the farm to build amazing sculptures. Some resemble Hecate. Others recall our recent adventures. When she decides to create a monster Shape-Shifter, using discarded pieces of metal and stone, Trist and Jafet help her move the heaviest pieces.

'Now our farm looks like an art gallery,' Nance exclaims as she knows a lot about art.

'What is an art gallery?' Trist asks,

'A place where only the finest paintings and sculpture are on display,' she says hugging Zumi. 'You youngsters are extraordinarily talented. I'm so impressed.'

The mascs spend any spare time they have mastering other skills. Jafet is collecting every dialect and language he can find on their Tablet, moving them into one complete dictionary and compiling a complete history of Terra. Trist builds lots of machinery that will help Bert run the farm more easily and efficiently. Then he goes on to build machines with extraordinary abilities, like being able to shift goods molecule by molecule.

There are other changes, too. Seems as if all our recent adventures have altered the way we treat each other. Every morning, Trist asks us how we feel and how did we sleep? Then he listens to our replies. He's stopped talking in short sharp sentences. He's even stopped teasing Zumi. Sometimes he acts as if he truly likes her.

The other day I caught those two giggling over a paper book. 'Just look at those pictures,' says Trist. 'You ever seen anything that gross?'

'Never!' Tears run down Zumi's cheeks, she's laughing so much.

Trist shows me a picture of what an artist thought people in the future might look like. I laugh along with them. The artist has drawn a figure with two head-antennae and six fingers. How wrong can anyone get!

Zumi too, has started noticing when people are being nice to her and responding positively. Yesterday I overheard her say, 'Pya's so thoughtful. She never leaves me to carry a heavy basket by myself.'

Jafet has stopped talking like a Universal dictionary. After working this hard, he's just too tired. Instead of, 'Would you mind passing the spade, that is, if you're not using it yourself, or it's not being used for something more important,' he'll yell, 'pass the spade, will you?' Also he's started sharing more thoughts and emotions.

Charlie and Rio are also sharing, and not just with each other. They hardly ever bicker. Charlie has stopped trying to boss Rio around. I overheard him say to Jafet, 'Even though we're twins, she's the smart one.'

'Surely not,' Jafet replies.

'Sure she is. She always got better grades.'

'That doesn't make her smarter,' Jafet protests. 'Maybe just quicker. He frowns slightly. 'What does being smart mean, anyway?'

Charlie laughs. 'My dad used to say that being smart was learning from what happens to you. Not making the same mistakes over and over again.'

Rio has long periods when she almost, if not quite, forgets to look sad.

Most evenings the six of us sit around the old wood stove listening to me play the piano and hearing Bert and Nance talk about what life was like when they were young.

Bert said, 'When I was your age, we would cycle three kilometres every morning to catch the school bus...'

'Nance, what's cycling?' I ask.

The old people glance at each other. 'City kids.' Bert shakes his head 'Haven't you ever seen a bicycle?'

Jafet says, 'Isn't that a two wheeled mode of transport propelled by someone pushing the pedals?'

'My, oh my,' says Bert. 'Sometimes Jafet... it is Jafet isn't it?'

Jafet nods.

'Jafet, sometimes I think you've swallowed an

encyclopaedia...'

'An encyclopaedia is a collection of worldly wisdom...' Jafet starts, only Charlie hits him and they end up wrestling on the floor.

We're getting on so well, I can hardly believe we're the same people who once never stopped bickering. Between chores and our newfound hobbies, Trist and I find time to jog. Sometimes the others join us. Gradually, our cheeks turn pink, our arms and legs get longer and stronger. My belly has shrunk and turned into a waist. I'm starting to grow breasts, underarm and body hair. Where once the hair on my head was sparse, it now forms tight curls that reach halfway down my back, where once I only reached Charlie's waist now my head comes to his chin.

The others are changing in similar ways. The other day Zumi got a terrible fright. Nance sat her down to explain to her about menstruation. 'It'll happen to Pya very soon,' she adds.

Both Jafet and Trist have grown a head taller than us fems. They're almost the same height as Charlie. Their voices are starting to break. Sometimes a sentence ends up as a squeak. They are developing soft hair above their lips. One day searching through a shed at the back of the house, Charlie finds a slab of plastic with wheels attached to the underside. 'It's a skateboard,' he tells us. 'Bert used to ride it when he was younger.'

He takes it outside and shows us how to use it. Skateboarding teaches us more about balance. Zumi, Trist and Jafet quickly learn to flip and roll. It takes me longer. Soon we spend every spare moment skateboarding.

But while we lead this pleasant existence, strange things happen. Once, passing a darkened window, I glimpse my old avatar. How come she's back? Did this mean we were being returned to our Cells? This is the last thing I want. Living in a tiny cell, doing everything via our avatars, never being with the other Hatchlings, never eating proper food, or jogging along a country road; seeing a sunset, or letting the earth run through my fingers, touching a tree, stroking Roth or feeling the warmth of another's body...

On no! Much as I'd like to see Tutor-Henny and always feel safe and secure, I never want to go back to my previous existence.

I close my eyes. When they reopen, my reflection shows dark eyes in a heart shaped face. No avatar. Only my imagination. But later when we're in bed, I ask the others if they've experienced anything unusual.

'No,' says Trist. Then he frowns slightly.

'Honestly Pya,' Zumi splutters. 'You're so we-ird.'

I know she doesn't mean to upset me, so I just smile. 'Jafet, anything happen to you?'

'No, nothing,' he mutters. But later that night, when the others are asleep, he touches my arm. 'Pya?' I turn to face him. 'Yesterday,' he whispers. 'I thought I heard *ComCen*'s voice.'

The breath catches in my throat. 'Was it?'

'Though I listened as hard as I could, *She* faded away.'

'And?' I prompt.

I just make out his shrug in the dark. 'That's all I can tell you.'

'What did *ComCen* say?'

'Something... something about *The Great Disaster* and *The Great Plague*... and that they're using Charlie and Rio's genetic structure to see if it is similar to ours...'

'Wonder what it means?'

He doesn't answer.

Days flow by. Bert and Nance are always kind to us and appreciate all we do for them. Our team is having fun, but the twins still aren't happy. One night when the rest of us are asleep, I overhear Charlie saying to Rio, 'Once things settle down, we'll go back home and find them.'

'But what if they aren't there?' Rio says mournfully. 'They could be anywhere by now.' As her crying drifts towards me, I feel very sad for her. For maybe the hundredth time I wonder what it's like to have a Mother, Father and a Hatchling called Emma? To be missing them so much the missing is almost too much to bear?

26

'Return of the Snouts'

I'm getting used to living in 'Utopia', and loving every moment of it, when late one evening we hear a sound that makes our scalps prickle.

Motorcycles!

Revving down the road.

Heading towards us.

Roth barks wildly. We race outside. Two motorcycles stop under a light thrown by a full moon. The two riders dismount. We see them clearly. Those piggy helmets are unmistakable. One rider is tall and broad. The other as wide as she is tall. Fobia and Nego. Where is Oomf? Then I remember a laser going off in the middle of the night and a cry as if someone was hurt. Poor Oomf. I know what happened to her. But as I watch Fobia and Nego get back on their bikes and head towards the farmhouse, there's no time to brood about Oomf's fate. Snouts have no concept of right and wrong. If those two have turned up to Utopia, what will happen to Bert and Nance?

We duck behind some bushes. Jafet whispers, 'We have to help them escape.'

We're almost too frozen to move.

Suddenly Zumi creeps out from behind a bush 'I'll go and get them,' she says and heads for the house. Ducking behind trees, we follow.

The motorcycles pull up. Engines and lights are turned off. We hear Roth barking like mad. A beam lights up the night. Roth whines and falls silent. Tears dribble down my cheeks. Someone kicks the kitchen door open. A light goes on. Through the lighted window, we see Fobia open the pantry to check what's inside.

We creep towards the house. Trist taps on the old couple's bedroom window. 'Bert... Nance. It's us.'

I can see them on the other side. We whisper for them to climb through the open window. Bert does his best to support Nance, but she's so frail, it takes everyone to help bring her out. And all the time we hear Snouts crashing about in the kitchen. Whatever they come across, they destroy.

Soon we smell smoke. As we help Bert and Nance across the lawn, flames leap out of the kitchen window and lick the roof.

Half-carrying, half-dragging Nance, we head for the bush. Glancing back, I see the entire house is on fire, and Fobia and Nego are leaping around it in some kind of weird

Snout ceremony.

We don't hang around to watch. Plunging through woody scrub, we knock into trees and stumble over roots. 'Not so fast,' Bert pants. 'Too hard... keeping up...'

Though it's dangerous to slow down, we can only do as he asks. I tremble at every sound. What if Fobia and Nego decide to follow us?

Suddenly I step into nothing and fall backwards. Then I'm bumping over earth and rocks, plunging on and on... never seeming to stop...

Just as I give up all hope... I'm sure I'm falling so far I'll be smashed into pieces and die... the way gets smoother. Soon it feels like I'm riding Slide Forever.

Then I realise... this is Slide Forever...

Somehow or other, I'm back in that funfair...

I'm gliding... slipping down Slide Forever...

Down, down, down I go. And just like the first time, just like the time before, there's nothing to stop me. Isn't this the slide that goes on forever?

I crash-land into something soft.

'Ouch,' Zumi yells.

'Ouch!' I yell as Trist fell on top of me.

'Ouch!' Trist yells as Jafet falls onto him.

We just stay there, our arms and legs in a tangle. It takes me ages to push myself out from under.

I sit up.

I hear Rio and Charlie just in front. They're laughing. But where are Nance and Bert?

As I sit there trying to catch my breath, the sky starts to lighten. I stare around in amazement. I'm on a hill overlooking a valley. Though I've never been here before, I recognise the valley in *ComCen*'s holo, the one we visited daily in our meditation. Only this time when I touch a tree, my hand doesn't slide through it.

This time the valley is real.

27

Terra 2

We stand up and brush ourselves down. Nursing scraped knees, bruised shins and aching bottoms, we set off for the river. We wander along a riverbank bordered with weeping willows until we came to a village. We head into a park along a path lined by shady maple trees that leads upwards until we reach a pool where huge goldfish swim from side to side, their plump bodies courting the afternoon sun. I smell the mingled scent of jonquils, narcissi and jasmine. Bird-song fills the air. Bees, birds and butterflies colour it. From here we have an excellent view of a main street straddled by a mossy stone bridge and a dozen roofs just beyond. Here are the same calm streets, the same cosy shops and houses I used to see in my daily meditation when I was back in my Cell.

We return to the village and I touch one of the buildings.

It's solid. This time the buildings are real. My hand doesn't pass through them. These buildings are not a holo.

They exist.

They're real!

We link arms and wander along the streets. This village is strangely empty. No people. Not anywhere. We look inside barns and sheds. Each is filled to capacity with food, clothes, machines and tools. I marvel at what I see. It seems that anything we can ever possibly want is inside. Each building is set up as if someone has just stepped outside a minute before.

But Bert and Nance have vanished. What could have happened to them?

'Wasn't there a famous wreck just like this?' Rio says nervously. 'When the 'Marie Celeste' was found, everything on board was perfect. Only everyone sailing on her had disappeared.'

We stay together and keep walking, searching for some hint of what might have happened here. No one dares move away in case he or she gets lost. Back on the main street we turn left until we come to a collection of houses. Open doors are an invitation to walk inside. One house is familiar. I lead the others inside. Yes, there's the big room with the comfortable armchairs, the staircase I know must lead to another room with a bed covered in soft white pillows, cushions and doonas. But this house also looks as if the owners have just stepped outside.

Rio cries, 'What do we do now?'

In answer Trist takes Zumi's hand and whispers something to her. She turns to us to say, 'Let's go back to the centre of town.' As we follow her down the street, I hear a distant murmur like a swarm of bees.

The murmur turns into a roar. The sky darkens. A vast shadow spreads over the village. I look up to see a gigantic spaceship, Its surface pitted with many, many holes as if it has been travelling countless millennia. It almost blocks out the sky before it halts directly overhead. An opening appears on one side. Stairs tumble out and descend to the ground. People step out. They move down those stairs, their gaze so intense, it's as if this is something they've long waited for, as if something they anticipated is just, just happening.

Next *ComCen*'s voice echoes over the valley. This time *She* doesn't mind-speak. Her voice sends shivers down my spine.

'Hatchlings,' *She* says. 'We have come to the end of our journey.'

Journey! What journey? What is *She* talking about?

'Now future generations will live together in peace and harmony. When you came down Slide Forever, this signalled our arrival.'

I glance at the others. Their mouths are open, too.

ComCen says smoothly, 'Sit down and we will explain everything.'

We six settle on a bench and wait for *She* to continue.

***

ComCen says, 'Three millennia ago the planet you know as Terra or Earth became totally uninhabitable. Since then humanity has been searching for somewhere safe to settle. But until now, whichever planet we reached was, for one reason or another, quite unsuitable.' Do I hear a faint sigh? 'Sometimes the fauna and flora weren't carbon based. Once we thought we'd found the perfect planet. But the native population would have had to be destroyed. Long ago we had learnt how destructive this is. So we were forced to travel further and further afield...'

I shudder.

Is it my imagination or does *ComCen's* voice fade into the loneliness of space.

'So only now can our precious cargo, the inhabitants of this spaceship, be down-loaded. However, our Hatchlings had no experience of life outside their Cells. They had to be trained to cope in different situations. To do this the Hatchlings had to learn how to cooperate. So a simulation exercise was set up. The idea was to introduce you to the exercise we called *Independence and Cooperation*.'

I shake my head in an effort to clear it. So much of what *ComCen* tells us is hard to believe. And so much makes sense. Is this why She pushed us into the Twenty-first Century? When I think back to how *ComCen* forced us to flee the city, how we had to cope with the terrifying Snouts, Weirwolf and Arachnida, how we nearly died through lack of food and hardship, how we had to fight the terrifying Shape-Shifter, my heart gives an angry thump.

All this time those people are coming closer. Some faces seem familiar. Suddenly I realise that these are the same people we saw at the Funfair. I glimpse an elderly couple and a dog. We spring to our feet, calling, 'Bert, Nance, Roth, we were so worried...' As we stand there hugging, so happy to see them, Roth licking us all over, I glimpse the Family coming towards us.

Rio and Charlie head straight for them. Watching their reunion makes me happy and yet sad. Now the twins will have less time for us. Maybe they'll no longer want to be our friends. I hear Rio say to Mother, 'You mean you were part of this, too? We were really travelling through space?'

'So it seems.' Mother replies. 'We and these other passengers were lifted from the twenty-first century.

Remember how we lost you fleeing the city?' Tears trickle down her cheeks. 'Father and I searched for days...' Her voice trails away as she hugs them both.

'But,' Charlie persists. 'How did you end up on this spaceship?'

Father says, 'All I can tell you is that one night we fell asleep. When we woke, we were on this spaceship. Only then were we told that we'd been picked up and our bodies frozen so we could withstand time and space.' His face creases with remembered anxiety. 'But we still didn't know what had happened to you.'

Charlie cries, 'That's because, well... because we were with the Hatchlings.'

'But... but,' Rio cries. 'Why did *ComCen* choose us?'

Jafet carols, 'I think I know. It's what I always thought. Weren't you and Charlie born on exactly the same day as us, only many millennia earlier?'

'That is correct.' *ComCen* joins smoothly into the conversation. 'After *The Great Disaster* and *The Great Plague*, Terra's best scientists created Central Computer, or what you know as *ComCen*.'

'What exactly are you?' I ask.

There's a moment's pause as if *She's* reluctant to answer. '*ComCen* is not one entity. For want of an easy explanation, this entire spaceship makes up the total that is *ComCen*.'

No one says anything. We're too busy taking all this in.

'As I was saying,' *ComCen* continues – is it my imagination, or does *She* sound slightly annoyed at being interrupted, 'Terra's scientists built this spaceship to search for planets where humanity could be resettled. To achieve our aim, we needed to compare the twins' DNA with our manufactured genomes.'

'You mean, to see if we were as good as the others?' asks Zumi.

'Exactly. One important way was to use children who were born at the same hour many millennia earlier and compare their capacity for survival. These youngsters had to have a similar genetic structure to our own Hatchlings.'

'So none of our adventures really happened,' Jafet cries.

'This was all a simulation.' Zumi is equally indignant.

'Not all was simulation,' *ComCen* testily replies. 'Your escape from the City was based on certain events that did take place in the twenty-first century.'

I gasp aloud. 'We were on this spaceship all the time?'

'True, all that you have recently experienced was only Virtual. Separately, our children had many and varied skills. However you had to learn to work as individuals and as a crew. You had to know what team spirit is all about. You had to learn empathy.'

I feel a sudden flush of anger. 'But it was all so dangerous–'

'Not really,' *ComCen* calmly replies. 'We would never have allowed you to be in any true danger. But to test your responses, it had to seem as if all these situations were in truth, extremely life threatening.'

I start to ask more questions, but *ComCen* continues, 'Each exercise had a specific aim. You had to meet the Snouts to understand how dangerous certain situations could be. You were sent to live with The Children to discover how difficult it is physically to survive in the wilderness...'

Trist buts in. 'What about Weirwolf?'

'And Arachnida...' Zumi calls

'And the Shape-Shifter...' I add.

'What about Utopia?' Jafet asks in a very small voice.

'Ahhh...' *ComCen* pauses a moment. 'Bert and Nance's

180

farm or Utopia as you call it, was to prove to both us and yourselves that you had finally completed the assignment and could come together as a team.'

I ask, 'What about those Snouts returning?'

'The Snouts were your final test to see if you could overcome your own need to survive to also think of rescuing a weaker individual. All these endgames were created to convince you that only if you work together can you overcome difficult situations.'

'And we were always on this spaceship,' Trist muses. 'We never lived on Terra?'

'That is true for you Hatchlings,' says *ComCen*, 'and why your Cells were so limited and you were so small.'

'What if you hadn't found this planet?' Jafet asks. 'What would have happened to us then?'

'You would have continued in much the same way as before,' *ComCen* says calmly.

I give a giant shudder. Living out our lives in those tiny Cells, never seeing each other, never knowing what it is like to breathe fresh air or walk on the ground. I cry, 'We'd have been better off dead!'

'Certainly, we would never have taken the risk of exposing you to each other's germs,' *ComCen* says primly. 'It so happens that only recently have we learnt to overcome that Great Plague mutant virus.'

'You mean,' Trist interrupts. 'We've never been in any true danger?'

'Not from our simulation,' says *ComCen*. 'Your true danger lay in not learning to work together.'

I think this over. 'And if we hadn't?'

ComCen's voice remains calm. 'Unfortunately, we were unable to reverse history. We had already eliminated all our earlier trials. Most unfortunate.' Do I hear another sigh? 'So even if this last batch of Hatchlings didn't work out, all we could do was start again.'

My eyes widen. Only now do I know what our true danger was. I give a sudden shudder. If we hadn't learned to adapt, our true danger lay in *ComCen* herself. Hadn't *She* emphasised that we had to learn to cooperate as a team? No wonder our tutors were never with us.

As I'm thinking this over, *ComCen*'s voice grows louder. 'However this time we have been more than successful. This time we have brought people that are multi-skilled and least likely to cause friction. Above all, our four Hatchlings will continue into the next generation. They are multi-talented. Pya has her music. Zumi has her art. Jafet can deal with ancient artefacts and dialects. Trist is a brilliant gymnast and technician. We will leave behind all the knowledge you need to set this planet up as a flourishing colony and make this land fertile. This will be a place where justice and harmony will always prevail. Together with the technology we have brought with us, Terra 2 will be a place where humanity will prosper. But you need to work as a team or you will once again self-destruct. For this you need Rio and Charlie. You need to learn enough skills to become leaders for future generations.'

'And did we... do we pass the test?' Trist's voice quavers.

'You certainly did,' sings another voice. Suddenly the tutors manifest themselves. I'm so thrilled to see Tutor-Henny, I rush into her arms. Of course I run right through her. When I look again, her face carries an expression I've never seen before. If I didn't know better, I'd say she was crying.

'Darling Pya,' she says. 'You and the other Hatchlings have a wonderful opportunity to make a fresh start.'

'But where are we?' Zumi whispers. 'What planet is this?'

'Would it make any difference if you knew?'

I say, 'Won't *ComCen* be here to help?'

'No.' *ComCen* speaks for herself. 'Our task is now complete. Our final instruction is to head into space to look for other unexplored planets and carry other Hatchlings there. However, we will leave you copies of all our knowledge. You must set an example to succeeding generations. It is imperative that you remind the future of past mistakes. This way, hopefully, no more Great Disasters can occur.'

Jafet cries, 'But I still don't see why you couldn't go back to try to prevent it?'

'Even if we could, what would be the point of doing that?'

'Well...' says Zumi. 'Couldn't you stop it all from happening?'

'Most probably the same mistakes would have occurred. History would repeat itself. No, you youngsters had to learn through your own experiences. This was humanity's only hope for the future. Now it is up to you youngsters to learn those lessons that will bring the best of Terra's civilisation to future millennia.'

At this the stairs slide back inside. The ship lifts and moves sideways. One minute it's here. The next minute, it has vanished. As we stand there blinking at the empty sky, I know a terrible feeling of loss. When I next look around, all our tutor-holos have disappeared.

What will happen to us now?

I should have known *ComCen* would never leave anything to chance.

'Now...' Mother holds out her arms. 'There's one thing that needs establishing. Would you Hatchlings like to come and live with Emma and Rio and Charlie?'

Would we ever. We follow her into the world of our dreams.

Goldie Alexander's books are published both here and overseas. She writes historical fiction, crime, science fiction and fantasy. She is best known for *My Australian Story: Surviving Sydney Cove*. Her latest work for Young Adults includes *Dessi's Romance, Lilbet's Romance, The Youngest Cameleer, That Stranger Next Door,* the verse novel *In Hades.*

For younger readers: the *A~ZPI Mystery series* and three collections of short stories: *Killer Virus, My Horrible Cousins,* and *Space Footy.* Her latest novels for this readership includes: *eSide*: *A journey into Cyberspace, Neptunia. Cybertricks, a*nd *Gallipoli Medals* and *My Holocaust Story: HANNA.*

She facilitates creative writing workshops and mentors emerging authors.

Teaching Notes and other details about her books can be found on her website: **www.goldiealexander.com**

NOTES for CYBERTRICKS

"It is the year 20,043 AD. Pya, Zumie, Jafet and Trist – known as the Hatchlings – live in tiny Cells, are cared for by their tutor-holos, and can only communicate via their avatars.

Pya narrates how the giant computer *ComCen* sends their real bodies back to the mid 21st (2043 AD) Century where they meet the twins, Rio and Charlie. But even if these six youngsters manage to survive in a very dangerous world, they must also achieve *Independence and Co-operation*.

Detailed Synopsis

Part 1. ComCen

Many millennia in the future, four Hatchlings live in individual Cells on Level 867, Circle 340987, Great Southern Continent, Terra. Pya's tiny Cell consists of a food-drink-tube, a wash-tube, and a sleep/chair. Because of the *Great Plague*, these youngsters can only meet via their avatars. Everything the Hatchlings do and think is monitored by *ComCen*. Other settings are merely 'holos'. All their waking moments are spent in school work and practicing '*endgames*'.

Though these Hatchlings are identical, they don't get on. Zumie is self-centred, and Trist teases her unmercifully. Jafet talks non-stop and never listens. Even the narrator Pya, takes little responsibility for her own behaviour. Having been told to study a 21st Century nuclear family – consisting of a Mother, a Father, a baby called Emma, and twins Rio and Charlie, the Hatchlings find themselves in a City in civil strife and being evacuated. Then unexpectedly, Real and Virtual come together as the Hatchlings small, weak bodies are moved into this new frightening world...

Part 2. Actuality.

Stranded in the 21st Century, the Hatchlings join forces with Rio and Charlie, to steal a car and make their way to the coast. From having been totally dependent on *ComCen*, now the Hatchlings must learn to walk, run, and care for themselves. After spending an uncomfortable night in a cave, they set off on foot to search for food, water and shelter – though still arguing amongst themselves.

Part 3. Bush-Wise

Eventually the six youngsters find their way to a bush-land reserve where there is enough food, water and shelter. However their tranquil existence is torn apart when savage 'Snouts' turn up. The youngsters escape, but are forced to join 'The Children', a group intent on returning to a simple existence. Life with 'The Children' means the constant threat of extreme danger, thirst and starvation, and working from dawn to dusk. It is when the cult's babies fall ill with possibly *The Great Plague* they run away. But before leaving Charlie steals Thomas' laser...

Part 4 Gladiators

Now they must battle the giant Weirwolf in a frozen Arctic waste. When they come to the village of Kroden they learn that not only has the giant spider Arachnida destroyed the village in but in a fit of jealousy she has also kidnapped all the women. There is a prophecy that only young girls can successfully outwit her. Pya and Zumie manage to do this by using wit instead of relying on outside help or strength. Now the Hatchlings are gradually learning to come together and work as a team.

Part 5. Cybertricks.

As their final trial, they end up in a futuristic game show where they must pit themselves against a Shape-Shifter, the most terrifying monster in the universe. Using their combined skills, they conquer him, and are sent to Nance and Bert's

Utopian farm where personal differences are finally ironed out. However, they must survive another Snout attack before they discover all these adventures were only to determine whether they are ready to create a better world.

In SCIENCE FICTION, the trend is that

1. it deals principally with the impact of actual or imagined science upon society or individuals. In this case the setting is many thousands of years into the future. (A.D. 20,043)
2. The story can describe something hard to imagine. eg. The Hatchlings live in separate Cells and can only visit each other via their avatars. They must be cared for by Tutor-Holos.
3. The story has some consistent internal logic. eg In 'Hatchlings' the internal logic is that humanity has almost destroyed itself and the few survivors can't meet in person.
4. The story can contain sustained characters with whom the reader can identify. Eg Pya, Zumi, Trist and Jafet quarrel and like each other just like normal youngsters.
5. The story contains believable characters. eg: Charlie and Rio. Bert and Nance.
6. The story can also contain extraordinary characters and situations eg. *ComCen*, Tutor-Holos. Weirwolf. Arachnida.

DISCUSS:

1. Describe Pya's Cell. Describe some of her daily activities. Describe the 21st Century City the Hatchlings find themselves in.

2. This story is not as simple as it might appear on first reading. There are several themes, mostly about what life might be like in a far flung future, but also what humanity must look out for if not to become extinct.

3. 'Cybertricks' is divided into 5 parts. As the story progresses, can you trace the Hatchlings efforts to 'come together as a team'?

4. *'So wasteful,' Jafet comments, 'when there are no fossil fuels or minerals left on Terra or the moon. They tried using nuclear energy, but there were so many accidents in the end they resorted to wind-farms, solar and sea-tide, though there was never enough to power to go around, this leading to trade wars culminating in the Great Disaster-'.* Do think this can really happen?

5. What is the REAL danger the Hatchlings were in?

ACTIVITIES:

1. Make a story-board or collage to show some of the endgames the Hatchlings must win.

2. Mock up an interview with Pya. Then change roles.

3. Interview Tutor-Henny. Ask her to explain her duties.

4. Illustrate five different covers for the five different parts of this story.

5. Draw a Cell. Show where the tubes slide in and out of the walls.

6. Draw a Shape-Shifter. Can you show how it morphs?

WRITING EXERCISES:

1. Design your own Cell. What does it look like? What tubes would you like it to have?
2. Write a story called I LIVE IN THE YEAR A.D. 20,043. It can be quite different from the world of this story.
3. Sketch a cover for your story.
4. You are trapped in one of the scary situations these six youngsters must face. How do you go about saving yourself?

DEBATE:

1. Humanity will survive long after AD 2043.
2. It is dangerous to try and fight some of the creatures in the Hatchlings' *endgames*.
3. Not all cults like The Children are bad.
4. Giant computers and Tutor-Holos can never exist in real life.

WHAT INSPIRED THIS STORY?

What if we are stupid enough to continue plundering our world and allowing global warming to the degree that too many people are left to starve and feel hopeless? It only takes watching the news or reading a newspaper to become sad about our future. I liked to imagine that even if things get to such a bad situation, that there is always light at the end of the tunnel and we will find some way out of this mess. I also meet too many children and adults who bully those they see as weaker and quarrel over nothing much at all. It's getting to know those kids that suggested the characters of the Hatchlings to me.

***

REVIEW by Sally Odgers

Pya, Zumie, Jafet and Trist are thirteen years old. Like any other children in their early teens, they take an interest in their appearance and in their peers. They squabble among themselves and chafe against the benevolent rule of their tutors. Yet Pya and the others are *not* typical children. They are Hatchlings, the cloned descendants of an Earth rendered uninhabitable by the Great Disaster compounded of war, famine and plague. And as far as Pya knows, they are the only Hatchlings alive today.

ComCen and the holo-tutors put the Hatchlings through their paces, allowing them to interact only as avatars, but sending them to many different places via Virtual Reality. *ComCen* says they must learn how to cooperate, but Pya longs for true bodily freedom from her tiny Cell.

Be careful what you wish for.

Stranded on Earth at the dawn of the Great Disaster on the 21st Century, the Hatchlings meet Rio and Charlie, who are also thirteen years old. That's when they realise how different they are. That's when they realise how dangerous this longed-for freedom can be. Separated from Rio's and Charlie's family, the six take a long and hazardous trek. The situation is bizarre, but the characters ring true. The Hatchlings struggle towards humanity as the human children try to adjust to the loss of their once-secure future. Has *ComCen* abandoned the Hatchlings? Is this some cruel game? As the shared experience becomes more perilous, Goldie Alexander keeps a firm hand on the reins of her story, moving the action from setting to setting, each one clearly depicted. The characters grow and develop, while the situation is always accessible. The author's eye is warm and compassionate, but she doesn't flinch from the harsh reality of an adventure where nothing is quite as it seems to the protagonists.

REVIEW by Anastasia Gonis

This terrific futuristic fantasy novel is set in the Great Southern Continent, Terra, in 20,043. Pya, one of four Hatchlings that survived the Great Disaster, exists in a Cell as do the other three Hatchlings, mascs Jafet and Trist and Zumie, the only other fem. All are nourished via food tubes and educated by , a super computer, while communication is conducted via their avatars.

Their Tutor-Holo is trying to teach the Hatchlings to work together cooperatively and independently. With this crucial end in view, and forced to face Reality, they are sent back to 2043 to exercise all they have learnt and to focus on working as a team.

Returning to the past where families existed, they meet twins Charlie and Rio, and the six children set out on a journey that will change them forever. While experiencing Reality, they must overcome great challenges, learn sustainability within many lifestyles, and slowly come together to understand the words of their tutor 'only through great effort and understanding can another Great Disaster be averted'.

All of Goldie Alexander's novels have positive themes of self-worth, personal improvement, environmental issues and sharing the world's resources flowing through them in subtle waves in one form or another. In this highly imaginative and well-crafted novel, many similar life sustaining themes appear. The leading characters are strong and powerful, and the weaker ones always evolve and improve by the end of the story.

Also available from Five Senses Education
by Goldie Alexander

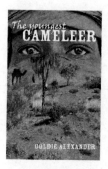

The Youngest Cameleer

Ahmed Ackbar, a thirteen year old Afghan and the 'youngest Afghan cameleer' speaks Pashto and a very little English. In late 1872 he sails into the prosperous city of Adelaide with three cameleers (Uncle Kamran, Alannah and Jemma Khan) to help look after four camels.

As the expedition treks into an unexplored interior, Ahmed must cope with Jemma Khan's enmity, his own homesickness, a very different culture and language, and the difficulties of exploration.

eSIDE

Sam and her mother Kate live in the rear of the Conch Café, close to Sam's best friend Melody and her dog, Billy. The building is owned by greedy witch Hecate Badminton who will do everything in her power to own the café's Good-Luck-Conch. After Hecate steals the shell and the café burns down, the girls have a series of adventures in 'eSide' where they must travel through dangerous digital worlds before they can recover their conch…

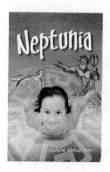

Neptunia

Cassie's training as a potential Olympic long distance swimmer is interrupted when she and her little brother Timmy are sent to live in a small country town without a training pool. Asked to deliver an important message to the water city of *Neptunia*, Cassie must overcome some terrifying monsters before she can complete her marathon swim.